C000142200

Dead famous

Dead famous

The final hours of the notable and notorious

Gordon Kerr

ONEWORLD

OXFORD

A Oneworld Book

First published in Great Britain by Oneworld Publications 2009

Copyright © Gordon Kerr 2009

ISBN 978–1–85168–677–3

Typeset by Jayvee, Trivandrum, India
Cover design by Edward Bettison
Printed and bound in the UK by CPI Mackays, Chatham ME5 8TD

Oneworld Publications
185 Banbury Road
Oxford OX2 7AR
England
www.oneworld-publications.com

CONTENTS

INTRODUCTION

Death is the great leveller. For all their wealth and notoriety, even the rich and famous have to meet their maker one day, just like the rest of us. Somehow, though, their endings hold a fascination that the deaths of ordinary mortals do not. Dylan Thomas and his famous 'eighteen straight whiskies', Mary Queen of Scots dressed in the colour of blood and wearing a wig, Ayrton Senna's last, terrible weekend – we are riveted by the ghoulish detail.

How often, when reading a biography, are you tempted to skip the turgid detail of the life and jump straight to the last few pages to find out about the last weeks, days and hours of the subject? *Dead Famous*: *the final hours of the notable and notorious* does just that for sixty extraordinary individuals, providing details of the last days and hours of the famous and the infamous, the dictator and the demagogue, the politician and the poet.

Whether their manner of dying took the form of a vicious shooting, as in the case of Albert 'Mad Hatter' Anastasia, or a quiet, dignified fade-out like former Beatle George Harrison; a controversy-laden demise as in the case of Diana, Princess of

Wales, or a much-mourned death doing what he loved best, as with the comedian Eric Morecambe, we are as fascinated by the deaths of the notable and notorious as we are by their lives.

Of course, where the notable and notorious are concerned, it does not stop with the shovelling of the earth into the coffin. Learn here about Andy Warhol's fabulous estate and the sale of his stuff after his death; follow the tortuous route of Eva Perón's mummified corpse during the twenty-four years between her death and her eventual burial; marvel at the meanness of crooner Bing Crosby towards his children.

Then there are the conspiracy theories that often surround the deaths of powerful people. We may not know who was driving the white Fiat Uno the night Princess Diana died; the part played by the Kennedys in the death of Marilyn may forever remain a mystery; we may never prove who bludgeoned *Hogan's Heroes* star Bob Crane to death with a camera tripod. But it doesn't stop us speculating.

— EDDIE AIKAU —

In the world of surfing, there are few stars whose legend is larger than the Hawaiian Eddie Aikau.

Born on the island of Maui in 1946, Eddie was the third of the six children of a truck driver and his wife. On weekends Eddie's dad would teach him and his brothers and sisters to surf on an old redwood board and, around 1959, Eddie and his younger brother Clyde carved out their own boards from marine ply and began surfing the Waikiki Wall, the birthplace of modern surfing.

On November 1967, Eddie arrived in the ranks of the great surfers when he dominated a field of top competitors in the huge waves of Waimea Bay. Pictures from that day appeared in *Life* magazine and Eddie Aikau became a star. In those days, however, surfing was not the wealthy sport that it is today, with substantial cash prizes and lucrative sponsorships. Eddie paid for his surfboards by working in a local pineapple-canning factory.

In 1968 he left the pineapples behind, quitting his day job to become Waimea Bay's first lifeguard. During the following three years, Eddie saved hundreds of lives. No one died when he was patrolling the thirty-foot-high waves.

During the 1970s, Eddie became the recognised king of big Hawaiian surf, winning numerous competitions. His private life was less successful, however, and a brief marriage fell apart in 1971. Eddie became troubled. Meanwhile, he was becoming increasingly intrigued by his Hawaiianness. Therefore, when the Polynesian Voyaging Society announced it was looking for volunteers for a journey of rediscovery aboard its double-hulled replica canoe *Hokule'a*, Eddie leapt at the chance. The *Hokule'a* was going to retrace the ancient Polynesian migration passage between Hawaii and the Tahitian chain, 2,400 miles south of Honolulu. *Hokule'a* sailed out of the Magic Island dock on the evening of 16 March 1978, straight into a strong north-east tradewind.

That night, however, the weather was bad and *Hokule'a* was struck by a terrific storm. She was tossed violently on the waves and finally capsized, the crew thrown into the raging sea and clinging for their lives to the upturned vessel. For hours they held on, watching helplessly as she drifted away from the shipping lanes where they might have been able to find some help.

Eddie had brought his surfboard on the voyage – it went everywhere with him – and he offered to paddle it through the rough water to the nearest land, the smallest of the Hawaiian islands, Lana'I, some twelve miles distant. It was a reckless, if extraordinarily courageous gesture. After all, one of the first rules of sailing is that you never leave the ship, even a capsized one. After much debate with his fellow crew-members, it was decided that he should give it a try. So, wearing a life jacket and armed with a knife, a whistle, a bag of sugar cubes and a strobe light, off he paddled.

A short distance from the upturned boat, the stranded sailors saw Eddie throw off the life jacket which was hampering his progress and paddle swiftly away across the choppy waters of the Pacific.

Twenty-four hours later, still hanging onto their stricken vessel, they were spotted by a passing plane and rescued.

As for Eddie Aikau, despite the largest air-sea search in Hawaiian history, he had disappeared and would never again crest the surf on the Waikiki Wall.

☠ POST MORTEM

- A memorial to Eddie Aikau was constructed at Waimea Bay Beach Park, where he had saved so many lives as a lifeguard.
- Every winter a famous invitation-only surfing event is held in Eddie's name – the Quiksilver Big Wave Invitational in Memory of Eddie Aikau, fondly known as 'the Eddie'. The twenty-four participants are made up of the most skilful and dynamic big-wave surfers in the world and the tournament is only held when waves reach a minimum of twenty feet; consequently, the event has only been held six times since its 1985 inception. The very first 'Eddie' was won, appropriately, by Eddie's brother, Clyde. Following his victory, Clyde claimed that Eddie's spirit rose out of the water

to meet him in the form of a large turtle that had surfaced just before his winning rides.

- The phrase 'Eddie would go' has often been seen in Hawaii, grafittied on walls or on bumper stickers. Eddie Aikau became a potent symbol of the resurgence of Hawaiian culture.

— ALEXANDER THE GREAT —

As action heroes go, there has probably never been one better than Alexander III of Macedonia, also known as Alexander the Great. The difference between Alexander and those other so-called action heroes, Sylvester Stallone, Bruce Willis, Arnold Schwarzenegger et al., is that Alexander did it for real; no stunt-men or body doubles for him. During his reign, he suffered at least nine wounds in battle, including a broken ankle, an arrow through the chest and a bolt from a catapult through his shoulder. He once temporarily lost his sight after being struck on the head by a stone. He was, quite simply, a great leader who, to the disgust of other, less courageous generals, unhesitatingly led his troops from the front.

On 29 May 323 BCE, however, the thirty-two-year-old Alexander was engaged in his second-favourite pastime after fighting – partying. He was attending a celebration in the Palace of Nebuchadnezzar II of Babylon, in honour of the death of the greatest of all mythical Greek heroes, Heracles.

Alexander had returned six months earlier from a victorious campaign in India, but recent bad omens and prophesies had clouded preparations for his latest initiatives – the irrigation of the Euphrates and a campaign in the Persian Gulf to settle the Arabic coast, due to begin on 4 June.

There were twenty A-list guests at the dinner, including Ptolemy I, king of Egypt, Perdiccas, one of Alexander's generals, Eumenes, the royal secretary, Philip, the royal doctor, Alexander's engineer, Nearchus, who had just been appointed Admiral for the Persian Gulf expedition, and Alexander's son, Peucestas.

During the dinner, Alexander displayed his learning – or perhaps his memory – by reciting an extract from *Andromeda*, a play by Euripides. Then he drank wine from the 'cup of Heracles' which was traditionally circulated at these events, toasting the health of all twenty men present. He filled the huge beaker with a large measure of unmixed wine (normally, it was diluted with water) and threw it back heartily.

Shortly afterwards, perhaps slightly the worse for wear, given the amount of wine he had consumed, Alexander decided it was time for bed. But he was persuaded by his close friend, Medius, to come and have a few more drinks with him. 'Great' or not, like most of us, he did not know when he had had enough and carried on drinking. Not long after, he left the party, drowsily taking a bath and finally going to sleep. You can't keep a good man down, however, and, before long, he was back drinking with Medius long into the night. Once again, Alexander had a bath and went to bed. By this time, however, he was showing signs of a slight fever.

Next day, the fever was such that he found it difficult to

walk and had to be carried out to perform his daily religious duties. Afterwards he lay in his quarters until sundown, issuing orders to his officers. Still shaky on his legs, he was then carried down to the river Euphrates and taken across by boat to the park on the other side where he rested. This was turning out to be more than just a monumental hangover.

Next morning, Alexander offered sacrifices, still issuing orders to his troops making ready for the departure to Persia. In the evening he managed to eat a little and went to bed, his fever mounting.

The following few days continued in this vein, Alexander slipping deeper and deeper into fever as the hours passed. By 8 June, his condition was grave, but in spite of his increasing weakness, he persisted with his religious duties and preparations for the imminent departure of his army.

On 9 June, he was moved back across the river to the palace. By this time, he was very ill and barely able to speak, although he was still able to recognise his commanders when they entered his room. For the next twenty-four hours his fever remained high and his soldiers became anxious. Rumours spread that he was already dead and that his guards were keeping it secret. They insisted on seeing their leader, forcing their way into his tent. As he lay speechless, they filed silently past him. It is said that at this point, fearing the worst, Alexander's commanders asked him who should succeed him. He is reported to have replied: 'Whoever is the strongest.'

Shortly after, towards sunset on either 10 or 11 June 323

BCE – sources can't agree on the exact date – the solemn announcement was made outside the royal tent that Alexander the Great, having conquered vast swathes of the known world during his twelve years and eight months' reign, was dead, aged just thirty-three.

☠ POST MORTEM

- Alexander was honoured as a god both in Egypt and in the cities of Greece.
- Ptolemy transported Alexander's body to the Egyptian city of Alexandria.
- Several centuries after his death, his golden sarcophagus was melted down by Ptolemy IX to make coins and was replaced with one made of glass.
- Many notable people paid their respects at Alexander's tomb, including Julius Caesar in 45 BCE. Augustus visited the tomb in 30 BCE, following his victory over Mark Anthony and Cleopatra and his conquest of Alexandria. According to a report by a Roman historian, when Augustus bent over to kiss Alexander, he fell forward and accidentally broke the corpse's nose. Emperor Caligula also visited and left with Alexander's breastplate.
- The tomb was closed to the public in the third century CE, six centuries after Alexander's death, because of the huge numbers of visitors and amidst fears that it would be damaged.

- Alexander's alabaster sarcophagus vanished during the fourth century CE.
- In 1995 a tomb was discovered in the oasis of Siwah. It was initially thought that it might be Alexander's but this view is now generally held to be incorrect.

THE CONSPIRACY THEORY

When Alexander died, it was not thought that he had been murdered. Six years after his death, however, it was suggested that there had, indeed, been a plot to kill him that night. In on the plot, it was claimed, were his friend Medius, Iollas his butler, Nearchus his admiral, Philip the doctor and others.

The plot was planned, it was suggested, by the Macedonian general Antipater, after advice from the philosopher Aristotle, who had been one of Alexander's teachers. Cassander, Antipater's son, travelled to Babylon in the last months of Alexander's life and is thought to have brought poison with him from Greece which he gave to his brother Iollas. Iollas, in his position as Alexander's butler, was perfectly placed to mix the poison into the royal wine. It was certain that Alexander would be the first to drink from the cup of Heracles and, on the night, everything went exactly as planned. It was reported that after the king drank, 'all of a sudden, he shouted with pain as if struck through the liver with an arrow'. He could only bear the pain for a few minutes before leaving the room where the party was taking place.

— SALVADOR ALLENDE —

At 7 a.m., on 11 September 1973, Salvador Allende, Marxist President of Chile, awoke to the news that two units of the Chilean Navy had rebelled at the port of Valparaiso, taking control of two of the country's three battle cruisers. Influential elements in the country had finally grown tired of his socialist policies – the nationalisation of American-owned copper multinationals and extensive land reform. Soaring inflation and widespread shortages, caused in part by a US economic embargo, had created an increasingly unstable situation and a growing economic crisis. Now it seemed the army and some of the people had simply had enough. Within half an hour, Allende was speeding towards La Moneda, the presidential palace, a cohort of armed police flanking his car during the hour-long journey.

At La Moneda, he immediately delivered a broadcast on the country's left-wing radio stations, urging the Chilean people to remain in their factories and at their desks. He went on to say that he fully expected the armed forces to remain 'faithful to their tradition' and to support the government by crushing the naval rebellion – a pretty forlorn hope, as it turned out, but he repeatedly insisted that he would not resign.

At 8.20, one of his Air Force generals called to inform him that a plane was waiting to take him out of the country. But, uncompromising as ever, Allende refused the offer and ordered him to do his duty.

At 10.30, the military junta broadcast an ultimatum, demanding that he resign.

By eleven o'clock, Allende had made the decision that the only way he would leave the palace would be dead and he announced this to stunned colleagues. Speaking to the Chilean people once more on the radio, he announced that he would 'resist by all means, at the cost of my life; to leave to the ignominy of history the lesson of those who have force but not reason'. This phrase reflected the Chilean national motto 'Por la razon o la fuerza' – by reason or force.

Things became even bleaker for Allende when it became apparent that not a single unit of the Chilean armed forces had remained loyal to him. La Moneda's civilian staff began to evacuate the building, leaving Allende behind, wearing a helmet and armed with a machine gun, personally directing the two hundred or so policemen who had stayed with him.

At noon, an aerial bombardment began and armoured cars surrounding the palace opened fire. It was struck by at least twenty bombs and was soon ablaze. Additionally, armed helicopters opened fire on the roofs and upper stories of the high buildings on either side of it.

Just after two o'clock, an infantry patrol burst into La Moneda's second floor. Arriving at the door, Captain Roberto

Garrido, commanding the soldiers, saw a group of civilians, armed with submachine guns, through the smoke. He ordered his men to open fire on them and one member at the front of the group was hit in the stomach, falling to the floor in agony.

Realising that the person who had been hit was, in fact, Allende, an excited Garrido shouted: 'We shit on the President!' Another burst of machine-gun fire followed, riddling Allende with bullets, and he fell back, dead. At that point another group of civilians burst in, pursuing the soldiers down to the first floor.

Dr Enrique Paris, Allende's personal physician, examined the president, finding at least six bullet holes in his abdomen and lower stomach. When he signalled that the president was, indeed, dead, a Chilean flag was produced and used to cover the body.

Allende's last words to the Chilean people had been: 'Probably Radio Magallanes will be silenced and the calm metal of my voice will not reach you. It does not matter ... I have faith in Chile and in her destiny. Others will surmount this grey, bitter moment in which treason seeks to impose itself. You must go on, knowing that sooner rather than later the grand avenues will open along which free people will pass to build a better society.'

 THE FUNERAL

Allende was buried anonymously, but, fifteen years after his death, in a 'gesture of reconciliation', his successor, General Augusto Pinochet, allowed a funeral to take place. The body was exhumed and placed in a new casket and, amidst great emotional outpouring, a memorial service was held in Santiago's cathedral.

☠ POST MORTEM

- Between 6 and 8 a.m. on the day of Allende's death, about six thousand leaders of towns, unions, farm-worker settlements, political parties and leftist cultural organisations were arrested throughout Chile. Prisoners were taken to military headquarters, interrogated and executed immediately afterward. The military described this as 'cleaning up the motors of Marxism'.

- Resistance in Vicuna Mackenna and Los Cerrillos was fierce, weakening only when the workers' munitions gave out. Mass murders in Santiago's working-class districts finally put an end to the resistance.

- It had been the intention of the military to tell the world that Allende had committed suicide. After the fierce resistance at La Moneda and elsewhere, however, they stalled for more than twenty hours. Finally, the news was leaked abroad and Chileans learned from foreign correspondents that their president had 'committed suicide'.

- The great Chilean poet Pablo Neruda died and was buried two weeks after Allende's murder. His funeral gave the Chilean people the opportunity to express their vehement opposition to the Pinochet regime.

- A four-man military junta, headed by General Pinochet, took over in Chile. Pinochet immediately instigated a programme of mass arrests and political assassination. Most of the businesses and farms nationalised by Allende were restored to private ownership. In 1989, Pinochet lost in a plebiscite on whether he should be allowed to stand in the upcoming election and was succeeded as president by Patricio Aylwin.

— ALBERT ANASTASIA —

Albert Anastasia was a creature of habit. Every day would start for him with a haircut in the barbershop at the New York Park Sheraton Hotel. Joe Bocchino had been cutting Anastasia's short, curly hair for years and as the mobster sat down in the leather chair, Bocchino, as usual, threw a candy-striped barber's cloth around him. On a chair next to Anastasia sat a manicurist and Jimmy, the shoeshine boy, sat at his feet, working on the big man's expensive wing-tipped shoes. Anastasia found it relaxing and on this particular day, 25 October 1957, he sat dozing quietly, a hot towel covering his face, perhaps recalling incidents from his astonishing life as people quietly busied themselves around him.

He had been born Umberto Anastasio – he would later change his name to save his family embarrassment as his activities began to make the newspapers – in 1902 in Tropea, a beautiful village on the west coast of Calabria in Italy. In his teens, he went to sea with his brother, Tony, jumping ship in New York, shoeless and without a single possession to his name. By his early twenties, his notoriously short temper had already got him into trouble and he was sentenced to die in Old Sparky,

Sing Sing's electric chair, after killing a fellow longshoreman. But when four prosecution witnesses mysteriously disappeared and others began to change their statements, a planned retrial had to be abandoned and Anastasia walked free. He had got away with murder.

Bootlegging during Prohibition provided him with his entrée to the world of the Mafia and he was soon working as a bodyguard for crime boss Joe 'the Boss' Masseria. He later helped Charles 'Lucky' Luciano as he rose to leadership of the National Crime Syndicate, taking part in the famous hit on his by-now former boss Masseria, in Scarpato's Italian restaurant on Coney Island in 1931. It was Anastasia who is said to have delivered the customary *coup de grâce* – a bullet to the head of the Mafia don, as he lay dying.

His skill with a gun and fearlessness next earned him the role of operating head of the syndicate's deadly enforcement arm, the notorious Murder Inc. Working with fellow psychopaths such as Louis 'Lepke' Buchalter, Frank 'Dasher' Abbandando, Louis Capone, Harry 'Happy' Maione, Harry 'Pittsburgh Phil' Strauss, Mendy Weiss and Charles 'Charlie the Bug' Workman, he personally ordered at least sixty-three of the estimated eight hundred murders for which Murder Inc. is thought to have been responsible. To his nickname the 'Mad Hatter', Anastasia added another – 'Lord High Executioner'.

By the early 1950s he had eliminated all his rivals in the Mangano family and had claimed top spot, a job he carried out with his customary ruthlessness and violent efficiency.

He began to get above himself, however, breaking the Mafia rule introduced by Bugsy Siegel that 'We only kill each other' when he ordered the killing of a man who had been a witness to a robbery. 'I can't stand squealers!' he exclaimed furiously, justifying the murder. He was also rumoured to be selling membership of his family – also in contravention of Mob rules – and stories of his terrible temper and violent instability were rife.

Eventually, agreement was reached amongst the crime bosses that Anastasia was getting out of control and the hit was ordered, being given to Joe Profaci. Profaci, in his turn, was believed at the time to have hired 'Crazy' Joe Gallo and his brother, Larry, to do the job.

As Anastasia sat daydreaming in the barber's chair, three men, wearing fedoras and dark glasses, crept into the barbershop, pulling out .38 revolvers and silently indicating to the barber, manicurist and shoeshine boy that they should move away from the chair. The three men placed their legs apart, crouched slightly, pointed their weapons at the dozing Anastasia and opened fire, shattering the early morning silence, until then broken only by the grumble of the odd car from outside or the muffled noises of a hotel going about its business. As the shots rang out, the gangster instinctively raised his left hand, in a futile effort to shield his head. The first bullet tore a hole right through his palm. Another couple followed in quick succession, one shattering his left wrist, the other entering his hip.

Anastasia had risen so far that he believed himself to be immune to attack and for that reason he no longer carried a gun. Old habits die hard, however, and he instinctively reached inside his jacket for the weapon he had carried all those years as he had clambered up the greasy pole. His hand clutched air. Around him, the sound of exploding glass filled the room as bottles of hair pomade and restorative potions were shattered by the fusillade of shots.

As the three members of the hotel staff tried to make themselves part of the walls of the barbershop, Anastasia was hit again, in the back this time, as he somehow managed to raise his large body from the heavy leather chair. His eyes were by this time empty, as if the life had already left them and he turned, reaching out with trembling hands towards the shooters as if he wanted to embrace them – or, more likely, strangle them. In his confusion, however, he failed to realise that it was merely their reflections in the mirrors in front of him that he was gesturing towards.

The striped barber's cloth still wrapped around the upper half of his body, he finally sank to the floor. One of his attackers calmly but purposefully strode over to his prone, crumpled body and delivered the *coup de grâce*, just as Anastasia had himself done all those years back to Joe Masseria – a single bullet in the back of his head.

 THE FUNERAL

Anastasia was buried in Green-Wood Cemetery in Brooklyn, New York, but he did not have the customarily extravagant gangland funeral. His family felt it inappropriate to ask for a Mass, given the life he had led. Instead, a wake was held at Andrew Torregrossa's funeral home in Brooklyn, but there was a low turnout and watching police were disappointed not to spot any mobsters, apart from old-timer Augie Pisano, who had also worked for Joe 'the Boss'. Anastasia was laid to rest in a comparatively inexpensive coffin, watched by his distraught wife, Elsa, and his recently graduated son, Albert Jr. The priest, who said a prayer and placed rosaries in Anastasia's hands, did not even travel to the cemetery and the funeral cortege was made up of just six cars – the hearse, a car for the flowers and four cars containing family members.

☠ POST MORTEM

- As ever with gangland killings, Anastasia's murder remained unsolved. Although it was said at the time that the Gallo brothers were the shooters, recent evidence suggests that the killers may have actually been Stephen Armone, Arnold 'Witty' Wittenberg and Stephen 'Stevie Coogin' Grammauta.

- Following Anastasia's murder, the chairs in the barbershop at the Park Sheraton Hotel were turned round to face away from the mirrors towards which he had reached out.

- The barber's chair in which Anastasia was attacked was auctioned off for $7,000 and was owned for many years by the late British-born American comedian and violinist Henny Youngman.

• The killings and betrayals continued.

 **THE CONSPIRACY THEORY**

Forgeddaboudit! It was the Mafia – everything's a conspiracy!

— JOHN BELUSHI —

By the early 1980s, John Belushi's drug intake was spiralling out of control, raising concerns amongst friends and associates who recognised a strong, self-destructive side to this larger-than-life character. Many concurred with what *Saturday Night Live* writer Michael O'Donoghue said of him around this time: 'The same violent urge that makes John great will ultimately destroy him.'

On 4 March 1982, Belushi was excited because he had finally been given the opportunity to expand his horizons and stabilise his career at the same time. It had certainly been an astonishing career, so far. Born in 1949, to immigrant Albanian restaurant owners, he had been a performer from an early age, achieving cult stardom through his brilliant performance in the 1978 film *National Lampoon's Animal House* and his appearances on NBC's top-rated satirical television show, *Saturday Night Live*. A *Saturday Night Live* sketch, *The Blues Brothers*, performed with fellow comedian Dan Akroyd, was made into a hugely success-ful film. In the debit column, however, were commercial fail-ures such as the 1981 film *Continental Divide*, in which Belushi plays a reporter investigating a corrupt Chicago councilman.

The source of Belushi's excitement was the offer of a serious role in the film *Once Upon a Time in America*, to be directed by the cult Italian spaghetti-western director Sergio Leone. Not only did it offer a chance to prove that he could handle dramatic roles as well as comedic, but, best of all, he would be sharing the screen with the one and only Robert De Niro. He must have been serious about it because he had even agreed to shed forty pounds for the part.

That Thursday night, however, Belushi was engaged in his favourite pursuit – having fun. He dined with De Niro on Sunset Strip, no doubt discussing the film that would bring their two talents together, before going on to a show at West Hollywood's Improv club in the company of his girlfriend Cathy Smith, a former backing singer with rock group The Band, and *Saturday Night Live* writer Nelson Lyon. Leaving Improv, the trio staggered to another club, On the Rox, where Belushi jammed onstage with Johnny Rivers. They then went to the Rainbow Room, next door. When Belushi began to complain that he felt ill, however, they decided to return to their hotel. People who saw John Belushi that night claim he was on a relentless cocaine high. Unfortunately, this was nothing out of the ordinary.

One of the others drove his Mercedes back to Bungalow 3 at the Chateau Marmont Hotel in West Hollywood, where, for the past week, he had been staying with Smith. He was helped indoors and once there, immediately went to the bathroom and threw up. That represented nothing more than a mere inconvenience, however, as he resumed drinking wine and inhaling and injecting cocaine. According to Smith, Belushi asked her to inject him with a needle full of drugs several times that night and, although normally terrified of needles, he seemed to be enjoying the high he got from it.

At some point in the proceedings, comedian Robin Williams, who was no stranger to cocaine in the 1980s, dropped by for a bit, but Williams was wary of Smith and wondered why Belushi was hanging out with someone like her. As he left, he joked with Belushi, 'If you ever get up again, call.'

Then, sometime after 3 a.m., De Niro is said by some sources to have knocked on the door but, taking a look at what was going on, quickly made his excuses and left. Meanwhile, the booze and drugs binge continued unabated.

Around 6.30 a.m., Belushi took a shower and finally, at around eight, he went to bed. Cathy Smith recalls that he lay on his right side, shaking and wheezing from a sinus problem. At 9.30, she heard him sneezing loudly and went in to check that he was all right. He told her he was fine. She gave him a glass of water and he went back to sleep.

Looking in again at 10.15 that morning, she saw that he was covered by a blanket and seemed to be sleeping. By this time, however, she was hungry. She took the Merc and went out to get something to eat.

At 12.30, Belushi's physical trainer Bill Wallace, who had been helping him to lose weight, arrived at the bungalow to find the actor comatose in his bed, lying in a tight foetal position. Wallace became concerned immediately because he knew Belushi was an inveterate snorer. On this occasion, however, he was not making a sound. Realising Belushi was in trouble, Wallace immediately cleaned out the star's mucus-filled nose, laid him on the floor and called for help.

The paramedics arrived too late, however, and at 12.45 it was announced that John Belushi had become a fully paid-up member of a clique that he had once joked about on *Saturday Night Live* – the 'live fast, die young, leave a good-looking corpse' clique. Sadly, in this case, the corpse probably did not look so good.

 ## THE FUNERAL

John Belushi was buried on 10 March in Abel's Hill Cemetery, on Martha's Vineyard. His fellow Blues Brother, Dan Akroyd, led the procession on his motorcycle and as it began to snow, James Taylor sang *That Lonesome Road*.

A memorial service was held next day at the Cathedral of St John Divine, in New York during which Akroyd played a tape of The Ventures guitar instrumental *The 2000 Pound Bee*, the fulfilment of a pact the two had made earlier in the year to play the song at each other's funerals.

In May 1983, Belushi's widow, Judy, had John's coffin moved to an unknown location in the cemetery, because fans were desecrating his grave. During the operation, John's wooden casket collapsed and a copper one had to be used instead.

☠ POST MORTEM

The coroner judged Belushi's death to have been caused by 'acute cocaine and heroin intoxication' but Cathy Smith admitted in an interview in the *National Enquirer* that she had administered a speedball – a mixture of cocaine and heroin – to the star. The authorities pounced and she was indicted for first-degree murder for her role in the injection of the lethal doses that killed Belushi. She fled to Canada and fought extradition until 1986 when she was convicted of manslaughter, spending eighteen months in prison.

— BILLY THE KID —

Born in 1859 in the slums of New York City, Henry McCarty travelled west with his mother, following the death of his father. They arrived in Silver City, New Mexico, in 1873 but by 1877, McCarty was in Lincoln County, New Mexico, going by the name of William Bonney.

Lincoln County was a byword for anarchy at the time. The indigenous Apaches had been tamed and cattlemen had now turned on each other, fighting for local power. Unfortunately, Bonney allied himself to the losing side, working as a ranch-hand for a rancher called John Tunstall who became something of a father-figure for the young man. When Tunstall was ambushed and killed in 1878 by a sheriff's posse, the legend of Billy the Kid was launched as Bonney set out on a campaign of revenge.

Patrick Floyd Garrett had been a buffalo hunter in Texas before drifting into New Mexico and being elected sheriff of Lincoln County in 1880 with orders to restore justice to the area. One of the first things he did was to arrest Bonney who had spent the past two years killing John Tunstall's murderers, Garrett's predecessor as sheriff and his deputy amongst them.

By the time the young outlaw was convicted and sentenced to hang, it was reckoned that he had killed at least twenty-one men.

But, while Garrett was away on county business, Bonney attacked his guards and escaped, shooting two men in the process and leaving town on a stolen horse.

Claiming that he had been promised a pardon by Governor Lew Wallace in exchange for information about other killings, Bonney escaped as far as a friend's ranch at Fort Sumner, about 140 miles west of Lincoln County. Garrett set off in pursuit, accompanied by two of his deputies, John Poe and Thomas McKinney.

On the night of 14 July, the three men approached the former fort that had now been converted to living quarters. However, the residents sympathised with the Kid and refused to provide Garrett with information. The sheriff decided to find Peter Maxwell, an old friend and the son of Lucien B. Maxwell, a New Mexico land baron. He thought Maxwell might give him the information he needed.

They rode towards Maxwell's property, stopped to unsaddle their horses, had some coffee and then went into an orchard that ran down to a row of old buildings, some sixty yards from Maxwell's house. Approaching these houses, they could hear people inside speaking in Spanish. After a short while, a man stood up. He was wearing a broad-brimmed hat, dark waistcoat and trousers and was shirt-sleeved. He spoke a few words, went to the fence, jumped it and walked towards a house.

Unknown to Garrett and his deputies, this man was Billy the Kid.

He entered the house – it belonged to a Mexican friend – removed his hat and boots and stretched out on a bed, reading a newspaper. Soon, however, he woke up another man who was asleep in the same room and told him to get up and make some coffee. He added that he was hungry and asked for a butcher's knife so that he could go over to the Maxwell house to get some beef. The Mexican gave him a knife and the Kid, hatless and barefooted, set off on the short journey to Peter Maxwell's house.

Garrett still did not recognise the Kid as he left the orchard. He and his men retreated a short distance and, trying to avoid the houses, approached Maxwell's house from the opposite direction. Arriving at the porch, Garrett told Poe and McKinney to stay where they were and slipped into the house.

It was close to midnight and Maxwell was already in bed. Garrett approached the bed in which he was lying, sat down on it and asked him in a hushed voice if he knew where Billy the Kid was. Maxwell told him that the Kid had been there but he had no idea if he still was. Just then, a man sprang quickly into the doorway, shouting in Spanish: 'Who's there?' When there was no reply the man stepped cautiously into the dark room, holding a gun in his right hand and a knife in the other.

As he approached the bed, Garrett leant down and hissed: 'Who is it, Pete?' But Maxwell did not answer. The intruder came close and leaned down, both hands on the bed, his right hand almost touching Garrett's knee in the darkness. He asked in a low voice: 'Who are they, Pete?' At that moment, Maxwell whispered to Garrett: 'That's him!' The Kid, realising there was another man present, raised his pistol about twelve inches away from the sheriff's chest. He then retraced his steps back across the room, shouting in Spanish: 'Who is it?' Garrett wasted no time. He drew his revolver rapidly and fired into the darkness in the direction of the words. Throwing his body to one side, he fired again. There was no point in the second shot. Aged just twenty-one, Billy the Kid was already dying as he fell to the ground.

 ## THE FUNERAL

William Bonney was buried at Fort Sumner and shares a plot with his friends Charles Bowdre and Tom O'Folliard. The grave actually has two tombstones; the first, erected in 1932, was purchased by Charlie Foor, a pall-bearer at the Kid's funeral. The second tombstone was erected in 1940. The main tombstone is inscribed 'Pals'.

 ## POST MORTEM

- Pat Garrettt was shot and killed near Las Cruces in 1908 in a dispute over grazing land. His body lies in the Masonic cemetery, Las Cruces.
- Garrettt's image is part of the logo on Lincoln County Sheriff's Department uniforms.

- Garrett's daughter, Elizabeth, wrote *O Fair New Mexico*, the state song.

 THE CONSPIRACY THEORY

- Ollie 'Brushy Bill' Roberts, originating from Hico, Texas, but living in New Mexico in 1950, claimed for years after the Kid's death to be William Bonney and demanded the pardon he had been promised by Governor Wallace.
- It is claimed that it was Pat Garrett himself who smuggled into the jailhouse the gun that Billy the Kid used to escape. This theory maintains that the body that was buried was actually a drunk called Billy Barlow who was shot in the face by Garrett and the Kid to prevent recognition. A man named Homer Overton swore an affidavit that he had been told this story by Garrett's widow, Apolonaria, in 1940, when he was just nine years old.
- Overton's sworn statement was offered in support of a failed move to exhume the body of Catherine Antrim, the Kid's mother so that her DNA could be compared with Brushy Bill's.

— KAREN CARPENTER —

In 1983, Karen Carpenter was living in a condominium in Los Angeles, fittingly at 2222 Avenue of the Stars, while her brother Richard, the other half of the phenomenally successful singing duo The Carpenters, lived in Downey, near the house they had built for their parents.

The siblings had enjoyed major pop success, touring the world and selling some eighty million records. Their personal lives were far from happy, however. Richard was addicted to sleeping pills and, for many years, Karen had battled with anorexia nervosa. In Richard's words, she had actually been a 'chubby teenager', but by the autumn of 1975, after years of gorging herself on thyroid and laxative pills and throwing up what little food she ate, she weighed only around eighty pounds. When she walked onstage, audiences gasped at how thin she was. She had to lie down between shows and that same year had collapsed onstage in Las Vegas while singing *Top of the World*. She was a long way from the top of the world when she was finally admitted to hospital in the mid 1970s. But doctors and therapists could do little to help her.

It was at her parents' house that Karen spent the evening of

3 February. She ate her last meal with them at Bob's Big Boy restaurant, in Downey. Somewhat predictably, she had a Caesar salad.

Next morning, she got up, put on a red jogging suit in the pocket of which was a vial of Ativan – a drug that belongs to the class of drugs called benzodiazepines, generally used for sedation and anxiety disorders. She went into the kitchen at approximately 8.45 and five minutes later her mother found her unconscious on the floor.

Paramedics were called and she was taken to the Downey Community Hospital where, in spite of all the doctors' best efforts, she was pronounced dead at 9.51 p.m. of a cardiac arrest brought on by the strain the anorexia had put on her heart. She was thirty-two years old and weighed just 105 pounds.

 THE FUNERAL

On the morning of 5 February Karen's body was taken to the Utter McKinley funeral home where, on the following day, 6 February, a viewing was held. Her casket was cream coloured and remained closed, with a photograph placed on top by Richard. The funeral service took place at the Downey United Methodist Church, and although only six hundred were invited, one thousand mourners turned up. Amongst those present were Olivia Newton-John, Burt Bacharach and Dorothy Hamill. The service was broadcast to the crowds outside and included an instrumental version of a Carpenters medley including *Rainy Days and Mondays* and *We've Only Just Begun*. Karen was buried in Forest Lawn Memorial Park, Cypress, California, her crypt bearing the legend: 'A star on earth – A star in heaven'.

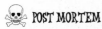 ## POST MORTEM

On 11 December 2003, Richard had the bodies of Karen and their parents exhumed and reinterred in Pierce Brothers Valley Oaks memorial park in Westlake Village, California because he had bought a new house there, putting a whole new meaning into the words of their hit song *Close To You*.

— EDITH CAVELL —

During the evening of 11 October 1915, Reverend Stirling Gahan, an English clergyman, visited the British nurse Edith Cavell in her prison cell and gave her Holy Communion. Although she had been condemned to death, and he was visiting her on the eve of her execution, he described her as 'admirably strong and calm'. When he asked her whether the confession she had made in court was sincere and had been made of her own free will, Reverend Gahan said that she had told him she was perfectly well and knew what she had done. She said that, according to the law, she was, of course, guilty, adding that she was happy to die for her country. 'I realise that patriotism is not enough,' she said. However, 'I must have no hatred or bitterness toward anyone.'

Her death sentence had not been pronounced in open court. Her executioners, in an effort to conceal from the outside world what was going to happen, came to her cell and, behind locked doors, informed her of the sentence – death by shooting.

Unfortunately, in pleading guilty to all charges, she had admitted that not only did she help around two hundred Allied soldiers to cross the Belgian frontier into neutral Holland; she had also received letters thanking her when the soldiers arrived in England. This was a serious admission – helping soldiers to cross into neutral Netherlands was one thing; helping them to reach England, a country at war with Germany, was another.

Throughout the night of 10 October, diplomats, including the American and Spanish ambassadors, attempted to secure a reprieve from the German military governor of Brussels, General von Sauberzweig. They urged that he contact the Kaiser, claiming that, as with the sinking of the Lusitania, her execution would seriously damage the German cause and do nothing but good for the British. The governor angrily refused their appeals.

At 6 a.m. the following morning, she was taken in a car with Philippe Baucq, also condemned to death for aiding the enemy, to the Tir National, the Brussels rifle range. Accompanying her was a chaplain, Pasteur Le Seur – she had been denied the presence of Reverend Gahan. Awaiting them at Tir National was a company of 250 men and a military court councillor, Dr Stoeber, the commandant of the prison, Captain Wilhelm Behrens, and a Dr Benn.

When Edith and Baucq had been brought forward, the sentence of the court was read out before they were allowed a moment with their clergyman. Le Seur took Edith's hand and gave her a blessing. She squeezed his hand in return and asked him to tell her loved ones that she believed her soul to be safe and that she was 'glad to die for my country'.

She was then loosely bound to the execution post and a soldier tied a blindfold around her eyes which, he later reported, were brimming with tears.

Each of the condemned had a firing squad consisting of eight men, standing at a distance of six paces from the victims. They took aim and the command was given to fire. Sixteen shots rang out and Edith and Baucq sank to the ground.

She had been shot through the forehead and blood streamed down her face, but horrifically for all present, she attempted to stand up three times with her hands raised, each time sinking to the ground again. After the third attempt, her body lay still. She had gone to her death wearing her nurse's uniform.

 ## THE FUNERAL

They hurriedly buried her at the rifle range, marking her grave with a simple wooden cross, but after the war her body was exhumed and taken to Westminster Abbey where a funeral service was held for her on 15 May 1919. Her coffin was then taken by special train to Thorpe Station, Norwich. She was taken in procession to Norwich Cathedral and buried there in a spot known as Life's Green.

 ## POST MORTEM

- Although the German action was justified according to the rule of war, the shooting of Edith Cavell was a serious blunder. Within days, the heroic nurse became a worldwide martyr, and the Germans were universally described as 'murdering monsters'.

- As a result of her execution, Allied morale was strengthened and recruitment doubled during the eight weeks following her death.
- She is commemorated in a statue near Trafalgar Square.

NICOLAE AND ELENA CEAUŞESCU

In Woody Allen's hilarious 1960s film *Bananas*, Allen, who has somehow become a South American dictator, announces that all men are from now on to wear their underpants outside their trousers. It would have come as no surprise if Nicolae Ceauşescu, who had become president of Romania in 1967, had made a similar pronouncement.

For instance, he banned abortion, birth control and divorce, decreeing that all Romanian women must bear five children apiece. As a result, state-run orphanages were soon filled to overflowing with about 150,000 orphans in a country with a population of only five million.

Ceauşescu's paranoia unleashed many other bizarre policies and practices on an increasingly impatient and confused Romanian people. He would only wear clothes that had been stored under guard in a warehouse; he promoted a labrador retriever to the rank of colonel in the Romanian army, giving it its own house, telephone and motorcade; he had all typewriters registered so that he could trace any abusive letters; and, after shaking the Queen's hand on a 1978 visit to England, washed his own with alcohol to rid it of germs.

On 16 December 1989, the dissident Laszlo Tokes, an ethnic Hungarian Lutheran minister, became the focus of a massive anti-Ceauşescu protest in the Transylvanian city of Timisoara. The city's inhabitants had been angered by Tokes's forced relocation, but before too long the mob's chants of support for Tokes turned into 'We want bread' and 'Down with Ceauşescu'.

Informed about the protest, Ceauşescu flew into a violent rage and began ranting about a plot against him, planned by his old enemies, the Soviets and the Americans. He sent in the army and violence erupted with more than a hundred protesters being massacred. Ceauşescu had miscalculated, however. The Timisoara revolt very quickly erupted into a nationwide uprising against the government.

To counter it and to try to regain control of the situation, Ceauşescu organised a pro-government rally in Bucharest. His plan dramatically backfired when the crowds at his rally failed to do as he wanted and they too began to protest against him on live television.

Fighting broke out in the capital between anti-government forces and the Securitatae, the national security force that was reported to have maintained almost fifteen per cent of the population as paid informants. Senior army generals and many Communist Party figures joined the protests and the tide quickly began to turn in favour of the protesters. The

Securitatae were swiftly defeated, in spite of a system of underground tunnels that had been built specifically for them under the streets of the city.

On Friday 22 December, Ceaușescu and his wife, Elena, attempted to flee in a helicopter to Iran, but it was forced to land. They were finally captured in a car about sixty miles from Bucharest

Swiftly brought before a tribunal, the couple were charged with genocide; armed attack on the people and the abuse of state power; the destruction of buildings and state institutions; and undermining and obstructing the national economy. They arrogantly refused to cooperate, claiming the tribunal had no authority over them. Instead, they demanded to be tried by Romania's Grand National Assembly, as the members of the tribunal were only ordinary citizens. 'You can shoot us if you like but we do not recognise you as a court,' the seventy-one-year-old dictator said. The trial proceeded, nonetheless, the dictator appearing calm throughout and even smiling occasionally, although his face was gaunt and unshaven. By contrast, Elena's expression was vacant. She stared blankly straight in front of her and failed to react even when her husband patted her leg in an effort to comfort her.

At the end of the two-hour tribunal, the prosecutor summed up the feelings of the Romanian people: 'Esteemed Mr Chairman, I have been one of those who, as a lawyer, would have liked to oppose the death sentence, but it would be incomprehensible for the Romanian people to have to go on suffering this great misery and not to have it ended by sentencing the two Ceauşescus to death. The crimes against the people grew year by year. They were only busy enslaving the people and building up an apparatus of power. They were not really interested in the people.'

The elderly couple were sentenced to death by firing squad.

When news of the verdict leaked out, more than three hundred soldiers volunteered to take part in the firing squad, keen to avenge the sixty thousand lives that had been lost during the Ceauşescu regime. Ultimately, only three were chosen – an officer and two privates – by lottery.

The Ceauşescus' last wish was to die together and at 4 p.m. on Christmas Day 1989, that wish was granted. As the couple was led out to their execution, Elena snarled at one of the soldiers: 'I was like a mother to you.' 'What sort of a mother were you, who killed our mothers?' was his bitter reply.

'The anti-Christ died. Oh, what wonderful news!' was the way one Bucharest radio announcer announced the executions.

 POST MORTEM

- The location of the tribunal and the executions was never made known, for fear of action by remnants of the Securitatae.
- The summary nature of the executions fuelled rumours that the Ceauşescus were silenced to protect others.

- There was some criticism of Romania's new leaders from abroad. The strongest came from the United States. 'We regret the trial did not take place in an open and public fashion,' said a statement. Britain, however, was more straightforward and even sympathetic. 'It was a civil war situation and the normally accepted standards of legality hardly obtained at the time. Although one may regret a secret trial, at the time it was not really surprising,' said a Foreign Office spokesman.

- An impromptu governing coalition, the National Salvation Front (FSN), proclaimed the restoration of democracy and freedom. They dissolved the Communist Party, transferred its assets to the government and repealed bans on private commercial entities and independent political activity.

- Elections were held on 20 May 1990 and Ion Iliescu, FSN leader, former Central Committee secretary and deputy member of the Political Executive Committee who had fallen out of favour with Ceauşescu, won the presidency with over seventy per cent of the vote.

— BRUCE CHATWIN —

When Shirley Conran had last seen her close friend, the writer Bruce Chatwin, on 31 December 1988, he had seemed to be functioning quite well and had even been able to work on his new novel. A fortnight later, however, when she returned to see him, he was in a bad way, incontinent, thin and exhausted by relentless coughing.

Three years previously, at a clinic in Switzerland, Chatwin had been diagnosed as HIV-positive – the first major artistic talent to fall victim to the disease. Nevertheless, he refused to acknowledge that he was, in fact, suffering from the disease, attributing his illness variously to a visit to a bat cave, a rotten thousand-year-old egg he had eaten in China, a fungus previously reported only in a handful of Asian peasants and 'a killer whale cast up on the shores of Arabia'.

But by the end of the year, it was becoming obvious that he was fading fast. He was living at Seillans in the Var region of France, but his wife, Elizabeth, had wanted to get him back to London to go into an AIDS hospice. Chatwin refused.

'He would not move,' Conran later said. 'His face looked like melted wax. He could just say "Granny" which meant the rubber ring for his bottom and "Burnie" which meant he needed the bottle. He had christened the pee-bottle "Birdie" because it was shaped like a Picasso bird-vase, but, unable to speak properly because of his illness, it came out as "Burnie".' Conran read him the Lord's Prayer the night of her arrival, climbed into bed with him and cradled his frail body in her arms.

He spent Sunday 15 January enjoying the warm sunshine on the terrace of the house. Having spent the afternoon with him, Conran carried him inside after the sun had gone down. He lay on a chaise longue and she knelt beside him. She told him she loved him and to her delight, but with a great effort, he replied that he loved her, too.

By 3 a.m. next morning, however, Chatwin's fingernails had turned blue and he had slipped into a coma. An ambulance was summoned and Elizabeth Chatwin accompanied him to the state hospital in Nice.

The other houseguests arrived in mid-morning and filed into the room where he was asleep on a steel bed, an oxygen mask covering his face. Elizabeth was booked into a nearby hotel and his brother, Hugh, was contacted and told that he should fly out.

Throughout the Monday, he was given oxygen, but on Tuesday Elizabeth told staff at the hospital that he was already dead. 'That isn't Bruce,' she said. 'It's a shell. They're making it breathe.'

Shortly before 5 p.m. that day, Hugh Chatwin arrived and went with Shirley Conran to pay his last respects. They then returned to Seillans with Elizabeth. The following morning Bruce was taken off oxygen and finally died at 1.30 p.m., aged forty-eight.

 ## THE FUNERAL

On 20 January Chatwin's body was taken from the hospital in an undertaker's maroon station wagon with a gold, felt curtain at the window and appliqué stars. He was cremated in a non-denominational chapel near Nice, with a Greek Orthodox priest officiating.

On 14 February a memorial service was held at the Greek Cathedral of Saint Sophia in Bayswater. Bishop Kallistos Ware surprised the congregation by announcing that Chatwin had intended to travel to Mount Athos in September 1988, to be baptised into the Orthodox Church. The entire service, apart from these words, was conducted in Greek. Amongst those present were Martin Amis, Paul Theroux and Salmon Rushdie. (That morning, before leaving for the church, Rushdie had received a phone call from a BBC news reporter, asking whether he was aware that he had just been sentenced to death by Ayatollah Khomeini for insulting Islam in his novel *The Satanic Verses*.)

Elizabeth took Chatwin's ashes to Greece and, with travel writer Patrick Leigh Fermor and his wife, buried them beneath an olive tree, close to a ruined Byzantine chapel dedicated to St Nicholas in Chora. They poured retsina over the hole and said a prayer in Greek: 'May the earth rest light upon him and may his memory rest eternal.'

🏴‍☠️ POST MORTEM

- Published the spring after his death, Chatwin's journalism, collected in the book, *What Am I Doing Here?* sold 31,688 copies, reflecting his huge popularity.
- Seven hundred pages of his personal papers, given a reserve price of a few thousand pounds, were sold at Sotheby's in 1989 for £14,300.
- In 1998, Bruce Chatwin's paperback book sales exceeded one million copies. He is published in seventy-two languages, earning more for his estate than he ever did in his lifetime.

— ANTON CHEKHOV —

Anton Pavlovich Chekhov, perhaps the most popular Russian writer outside his own country, had suffered from tuberculosis since his early teens.

In 1904, aged forty-four, Chekhov travelled to Europe, accompanied by his wife Olga Knipper, a star of the Moscow Arts Theatre, to fight the increasing ravages of his illness. They stayed at the Sommer Hotel in the health resort of Badenweiler in Southern Germany's Black Forest and employed the services of a local German doctor named Schwoerer.

Coincidentally, two young Russian brothers, acquaintances of the Chekhovs, were also staying at the hotel. Leo Rabeneck was a student whose brother had fallen ill in Berlin when the two were en route from Moscow to Switzerland. A doctor had recommended a period of convalescence in Badenweiler and the brothers had taken rooms at the Sommer hotel. Recognising Olga Knipper at breakfast one day, they recalled that they had been guests, at the same time as the Chekhovs, at Lyubimovka, the estate of Stanislavsky, the great Russian theatre director.

Olga invited the brothers to drop in on her husband who,

she told them, was 'very homesick for Russia and for the company of his fellow countrymen'. However, in spite of her claims that her husband's health was improving, when Leo Rabeneck visited the writer he noticed that although the playwright looked quite well – he had good colour and was even slightly sunburnt – he seemed absolutely exhausted. He recalled later that the sick man coughed frequently and spat into a small spittoon which he carried in the pocket of his jacket.

Chekhov remained optimistic about his condition, even making plans for his return to Russia, but his restlessness soon began to show. On 29 June, he wrote to his sister Masha: 'I just can't get used to German silence and calm ... I've got a tremendous longing to go to Italy.'

Not long after, however, a heatwave struck southern Europe – the worst weather for a man in the grip of advanced tuberculosis – and on 12 July, Chekhov was struck by the first of two heart attacks. Even then, he seemed to rally. On the evening of Thursday 14 July, however, events began to move rapidly.

Rabeneck was resting after a walk in the hills around Badenweiler when he heard Olga calling him. She asked him to go and fetch Doctor Schwoerer who arrived to find Chekhov breathing with such difficulty that he had to be given oxygen. As he was doing this, Schwoerer whispered to Rabeneck to go downstairs and fetch a bottle of champagne from the hall porter. In those days, in that part of the world, it was medical etiquette for a doctor to offer the patient champagne when all hope was gone.

When the champagne arrived, Chekhov sat up in bed and gasped: 'Ich sterbe!' – 'I am dying!' The doctor poured out an almost full glass and gave it to the writer who smiled and said: 'I haven't drunk champagne in a long time.' He downed the liquid in one gulp and the doctor handed the empty glass to Rabeneck. As Rabeneck turned to place the glass on the table, he heard a sound come from Chekhov's throat, a sound he later described as 'rather like the noise a water-tap makes when air gets into it'.

It was only when the doctor let the writer's hand fall that Rabeneck realised that Anton Pavlovich Chekhov was finally dead, aged forty-four.

 ## THE FUNERAL

Chekhov's remains were locked up in a refrigerated train carriage marked 'Oyster Wagon' and shipped back to Russia from Germany for burial.

It was a celebrity funeral. The writer Maxim Gorky was there at the Novodeviche Monastery in Moscow with Chekhov's sister Masha, and his widow. He wrote: 'I am so depressed by this funeral ... as if I was smeared by sticky, foul-smelling filth ... People climbed trees and laughed, broke crosses and swore as they fought for a place. They asked loudly, "Which is the wife? And the sister? Look, they're crying ..."' The singer Chaliapin burst into tears and cursed: 'And he lived for these bastards, he worked, taught, argued for them.'

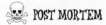

- When he died, Chekhov's body had not been laid out correctly and in the morning, rigor mortis having established itself, Rabeneck and Dr Schwoerer were unable to straighten it, the writer's head remaining slightly turned to one side.

- In order not to upset the hotel's other guests, the body was not removed to a local chapel until the next night. Instead of a stretcher, a laundry basket was used but it was too short for the writer's body to lie flat. Consequently, he had to be put in it in a half-sitting position. Rabeneck wrote, 'I walked behind the men carrying the body. Light and shade from the burning torches flickered and leaped over the dead man's face, and at times it seemed to me as if Chekhov was scarcely perceptibly smiling at the fact that, by decreeing that his body should be carried in a laundry basket, Fate had linked him with humour even in death.'

— PATSY CLINE —

Patsy Cline had flown to Kansas City to perform her special brand of country music at a concert to raise money for the family of disc jockey 'Cactus' Jack Call, who had recently died in a car accident. Perhaps she had been persuaded to perform by the fact that the thirty-year-old singer had, herself, almost died in a car crash several years previously.

The day after the concert, however, Monday 4 March 1966, Patsy was not feeling good. She had been awake all night coughing and a friend had persuaded her to ride back to Nashville with her and her husband in their station wagon instead of flying back in the single-engine Piper Commanche PA-24 owned by her manager, Randy Hughes. He had flown her to Kansas from Nashville a few days previously. She even brought her bags down to the hotel lobby, ready to load into the car but she had then abruptly changed her mind. Claiming she felt a sense of loyalty to Hughes she told her friends she would, after all, be flying back home.

But, that day, the storms that were raging in across the plains, were of such severity that the little plane was prevented from taking off. Their departure was postponed until the next day when, at around 1.30 p.m., Patsy, Randy Hughes and fellow performers Hawkshaw Hawkins and Cowboy Copas boarded the flight.

By 5 p.m., when the plane made a refuelling stop at Dyersburg Municipal Airport, a small airport in north-west Tennessee, they had already had to land and take off several times due to the weather, once being buffeted by a severe hailstorm. The Federal Aviation Authority was describing the weather as 'extremely turbulent' and thunderstorms had passed over the airport in mid-afternoon, more following just before the Piper Comanche had landed. The airport's operators, Bill and Evelyn Braese, both veteran pilots, urged them not to continue their journey. Bill Braese even offered them the airport courtesy car and offered to fly their plane to Nashville next day when the weather had improved.

But Patsy was keen to get back to Nashville, and while she, Copas and Hawkins headed for the airport restaurant, inside the terminal building, Hughes put in an order for fuel. In the restaurant, Patsy drank an iced tea and ate shrimp salad. Onlookers spotted her wearing a red trouser suit and her great hit *Crazy* was playing on the jukebox. It would be the last song she heard.

Meanwhile, Hughes phoned his wife to be told that the weather in Nashville was fine. Unfortunately, it was fine only because Nashville was in the eye of a storm.

The plane took off again at 6.07 p.m., but even without the storm, this would have been something of a gamble, because by that time in March it was already beginning to get dark. Fatally, Randy Hughes was not trained to fly in the dark.

Seventy miles west of Nashville, above Camden, Tennessee, Hughes lost visibility, and the plane started to nosedive. Investigators surmised that he was trying to land on a nearby highway, but the aircraft hit some trees on the way down and crashed in a hollow in a wooded area called Fatty Bottom, just west of Camden, probably at a speed of between 220 and 260 miles per hour. Patsy Cline and her three travelling companions were killed instantly.

 ## THE FUNERAL

Patsy's husband, Charlie Dick, brought her body home for viewing in a closed casket in her living room and a prayer service, attended by twenty-five thousand people, was held for all four victims on Thursday 7 March. Patsy was buried on Sunday 10 March in Shenandoah Memorial Park in her home-town of Winchester, Virginia.

 ## POST MORTEM

- The plane was found by William Jeffrey Holdsworth and his son, Jeners. Wreckage was strewn over a 250-yard area and as word spread of its location, hundreds of onlookers converged on the area, looking for souvenirs and carrying off personal effects. By the Sunday, three thousand people had visited the scene and one report says someone even took away a shoe with a human foot still in it.

- Randy Hughes and country superstar Jim Reeves had taken lessons from the same flight instructor. A year after the Patsy Cline crash, Reeves was killed in identical circumstances.
- Friends claimed later that Patsy had premonitions of her death, saying that she did not expect to live to the age of thirty. Shortly before her death she had established a trust fund for her children.
- An inscribed boulder marks the sight of the crash.
- When two pieces of the plane were recently put up for auction on eBay, the bidding reached $51,100 before complaints persuaded the website to pull the auction.

— BOB CRANE —

On 28 June 1978, Bob Crane, was playing the Windmill Dinner Theatre in Scottsdale, Arizona, the latest leg of his tour with the play *Beginner's Luck*. It had been seven years since the credits had rolled for the last time on *Hogan's Heroes*, the phenomenally successful World War Two prison camp comedy in which he had played the starring role. They had been difficult years. His *Bob Crane Show* had been terminated after only three months and a couple of films he had starred in for Disney, *Superdad* and *Gus*, had flopped miserably.

Crane had bought the rights to *Beginner's Luck* in 1973. He produced it and starred in it, and was taking it on tour around the entire country. As ever, he was carousing with his old friend John Carpenter, a video equipment sales clerk he had known for years. They had been introduced while Crane was in *Hogan's Heroes* and shared a mutual interest in topless bars and strip clubs, Crane's particular penchant being for buxom women.

As if his love life was not complicated enough, an affair with Cynthia Lynn, the actress who had played Colonel Klink's secretary in *Hogan's Heroes*, was followed by a fling with another actress, Patti Olsen, which had led to him walking out on his marriage of twenty-one years. Now, in 1978, he was in the process of divorcing Patti.

Carpenter loved it when Crane came to town. The actor's fame was like a magnet for women and once they had hit the bars and nightclubs and picked up a couple of women, they were in the habit of taking them back to Crane's apartment and filming themselves having sex. All was not well, however, by June 1978 and Crane had decided to call time on his friendship with the video salesman, especially as he believed that Carpenter had recently made a pass at him.

On this particular Wednesday night, after finishing his evening performance and signing autographs, Crane returned to his apartment with Carpenter. There he received a phone call from his estranged wife. They argued loudly.

The two men then went to a local bar where they had arranged to meet a couple of women. At about two in the morning, the four repaired to the Safari coffee shop, Carpenter leaving about thirty minutes later to pack for his return trip to Los Angeles the following morning. Carpenter called Crane from his hotel room and it is thought that it was during this phone call that Crane, tiring of the heavy partying and hangers-on, told Carpenter that he would not be seeing him again.

Next morning, Crane's co-star in *Beginner's Luck*, Victoria Berry, arrived at his apartment. There was no reply to her knocking and, the door being unlocked, she let herself in. Entering the bedroom, she saw Crane in bed, clad only in boxer shorts and so badly beaten that he was unrecognisable. He was also very dead.

'At first, I thought it was a girl with long dark hair,' she said, 'because all the blood had turned real dark. I thought "Oh, Bob's got a girl here. Now where's Bob?..." I thought, "Well, she's done something to herself. Bob has gone to get help".' Then Berry realised that it was not hair, but blood. 'The whole wall was covered from one end to the other with blood. And I just sort of stood there and I was numb. He was curled up in a foetus position, on his side, and he had a cord tied around his neck in a bow.'

He had been bludgeoned to death and around his neck, the killer had placed an electric cord.

Bob Crane was forty-nine years old.

THE FUNERAL

Bob Crane was buried in Oakwood Cemetery, in Chatsworth, California. *Hogan's Heroes* co-stars Larry Hovis, Robert Clary and Leon Askin attended.

His body was exhumed and moved to Westwood Memorial Park by his second wife, Patti, without telling Crane's children. There is a rumour that he was divorcing her so that he could go back to his first wife, the children's mother. He lay in an unmarked grave until 2003.

POST MORTEM

- Neighbours are reported to have heard nothing and there were no signs of a struggle, leading police to believe that Crane was asleep when attacked.

- Video equipment and a library of videos were found in the apartment showing Crane and Carpenter engaged in group sex with different women.
- Police described it as 'a well-planned murder', their investigation immediately focusing on Carpenter who was one of the last people to see Crane alive. He also phoned the apartment from Los Angeles while the police were there and was told that they were investigating an incident. Strangely, Carpenter did not ask what kind of incident. Blood matching Crane's, a rare blood type, was found in the car that Carpenter had rented. However, in the days before DNA matching, it was hard to prove that it was Crane's and the county attorney did not wish to proceed with a prosecution against Carpenter. The police were later accused of mismanaging the investigation.
- Under 'Cause of death' on Crane's death certificate is written simply 'Head Injury'.
- Fourteen years after the murder, in 1992, it was determined that fat tissue found in Carpenter's rental car was a match for that found in the apartment. The police also decided that Crane was killed with a camera tripod that was visible in the videotapes, but had been missing from the apartment when Crane's body was found. Charges were brought against Carpenter, but he was acquitted.
- John Carpenter died in 1998, still denying any involvement in Bob Crane's death.
- Crane died a wealthy man, having secured a percentage of *Hogan's Heroes'* revenues.

THE CONSPIRACY THEORY

- Bob Crane was a light sleeper, and there were no signs of forced entry. The County Medical Examiner surmised, therefore, that Crane knew his killer, that it was someone who had been there earlier and had re-entered the apartment through a door or window that he had left unlocked.

- There was cash in Crane's wallet, suggesting that robbery was not the motive.

- Due to the coldness of the body and the onset of rigor mortis, the Medical Examiner stated that Crane had been killed in the early morning.

- There was a bottle of Scotch on the table; Crane never touched Scotch.

- There were rumours that Carpenter had borrowed $15,000 from the actor and Crane was now demanding repayment of the loan.

- The killer had to be very strong as the lack of blood on the ceiling suggested a short swing of the murder weapon. A larger arc would have been required by a weaker person and blood would have been sprayed out from the wound.

- One theory suggests that a jealous boyfriend or husband of one of Crane's conquests murdered him.

- A tyre on Crane's car was tampered with during his last performance that night. It is thought that it was intended to strand him in the dark theatre car park where he would be attacked.

— JOAN CRAWFORD —

By 1970, Joan Crawford had done just about everything a Hollywood screen goddess could be expected to do. A stellar career, complete with Academy Awards, followed by burnout – she was described as 'box-office poison' – followed by dramatic comeback; four marriages, one of them to Douglas Fairbanks Jr; an affair with James Stewart; the bitch-war with Bette Davis; the marriage to the chairman of Pepsi and the board position after his demise; the rumours about her bisexuality; the miscarriages; the adoptions ...

Now, however, the parts had dried up, especially after her last, disastrous film *Trog*, described by one critic as 'worse than bad'. She turned up at a party for Rosalind Russell in 1974 and then the erstwhile Lucille Fay LeSueur disappeared from public view, taking to retirement and seclusion in an apartment on the twenty-second floor of Imperial House on New York's Upper East Side.

By 1977, Joan knew the end was not far away. On his death, she had replaced her beloved poodle, Clicquot, with a shi-tzu, Princess Lotus Blossom. But two days before her death, too ill to look after her, she gave the dog away to friends. Bedridden for months, she was suffering from cancer of the pancreas and also had serious heart problems. She weighed just eighty-five pounds.

In the last years of her life she had become a Christian Scientist and every day she was visited by a Christian Science practitioner who prayed with her and read to her from the writings of Mary Baker Eddy. Having dismissed her maid, Mamacita, the previous week, she was being cared for by a couple of loyal fans.

That last day, Tuesday 10 May – coincidentally the twenty-second anniversary of her marriage to Alfred Steele, chairman of Pepsi Cola – one of these fans arrived at apartment 22-H at around 8 a.m. She realised very quickly that the star was fading fast and began to pray. Joan overheard her. 'Dammit!' she exclaimed, 'Don't you dare ask God to help me!'

With that, she had a heart attack and died.

 ## THE FUNERAL

Joan Crawford's funeral took place on Friday 13 May 1977, at the Frank Campbell Funeral Home. She was embalmed and then cremated, the urn being placed on a pedestal in the chapel while a Christian Scientist read the service. Myrna Loy, Van Johnson and Andy Warhol were present.

Her urn was put with her husband's at Ferncliff Cemetery and on 16 May, Pepsi held a memorial service for her in New York to which, besides Joan's children, Anita Loos, Geraldine Brooks, Cliff Robertson and Pearl Bailey turned up.

A minute's silence was called for on all Hollywood lots the Friday after her death.

Another memorial service was held on 24 June in the Sam Goldwyn Theatre at the Academy of Motion Picture Arts and Sciences, attended by John Wayne, Robert Young, Myrna Loy and Stephen Spielberg. Jack Jones sang *Everything I Have is Yours* from Joan's 1933 film *Dancing Lady*. Delivering the eulogy, the great Hollywood director George Cukor said: 'She was the perfect image of the movie star ... I thought Joan Crawford would never die. Come to think of it, as long as celluloid holds together and the word "Hollywood" means anything to anyone, she never will.'

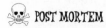 POST MORTEM

- Joan cut her children Christina and Christopher out of her will. It is said that she knew about the book Christina was writing – *Mommie Dearest*, a scathing account of an abused childhood, published in 1978 and eventually made into a film starring Faye Dunaway. The children sued and got a settlement of $55,000. Interestingly, Joan's other adopted children said that the picture of Joan given in *Mommie Dearest* was inaccurate.

- In November 1998, when *Mommie Dearest* was republished, Christina hired a drag queen that looked like Joan to accompany her to book signings.

- At an auction of Joan's personal effects in 1978, Andy Warhol bought her false eyelashes.

 THE CONSPIRACY THEORY

- Several of Joan Crawford's friends as well as Fred Lawrence Guiles' biography, *Joan Crawford; The Last Word,* claimed that she committed suicide. They pointed to the way she gave away a great many of her possessions as well as her dog in the months and days before her death. The coroner said that he had no reason to doubt that she died of heart failure but her friends base their suspicions on the facts that there was no autopsy and that she was cremated. There was, therefore, no evidence.

- In 1975, Joan had received an anonymous phone call saying: 'I will kill you. You won't know where or when, but I will get you.' She called in the police and the FBI and her apartment was under surveillance for months. She had sophisticated locks and alarms installed and her bedroom door was bolted every night. She was so terrified she did not set foot outside her apartment in the last eighteen months of her life.

— BING CROSBY —

Bing Crosby's astonishing career had begun to wind down as the austere 1950s morphed into the swinging sixties. By the time the 1960s had drawn to a close this most prolific of recording artists had stopped recording altogether and, by then, it had been many years since he had toured. In 1973, however, a health scare seemed to galvanise the elderly crooner back into action. He had been taken to hospital suffering from chest pains and fever and a tumour had been removed from his left lung.

To the great joy of his millions of fans, Bing began to record and perform live again. But his health suffered another setback when, in March 1977, during a televised concert celebrating his fiftieth year in show business, he fell backwards into the orchestra pit, rupturing a disc and staying in hospital for a month. He was soon back on the road again, however, appearing in Europe and taping a Christmas special, somewhat incongruously starring the androgynous rock star David Bowie, in England. Following that, he recorded what was to be his last album, *Seasons*. A two-week engagement at the London Palladium followed and then a concert in Brighton on 10

October, his last ever live appearance. Next day, he guested on the Alan Dell radio show on the BBC, singing eight songs. He finished the day with a photo shoot for the cover of *Seasons*.

On the twelfth, Bing flew to Spain where he planned to play golf and do a little hunting. Thus, on 14 October he and a partner were taking on a couple of Spanish golf pros at the La Morajela golf course near Madrid. A doctor in England had told Bing that he should only play nine holes of golf due to his ill health, but on this day he had decided to play the whole eighteen.

He played well, too, shooting a very credible eighty-five, as he and his partner won the match after handicaps had been taken into consideration. After sinking his last putt, at around 6.30 p.m., he bowed to the other players' applause and said, 'That was a great game of golf, fellers'. As they stepped off the eighteenth green, however, Bing suddenly collapsed, banging his head on the red brick path on which they were walking, raising an ugly bruise. His golfing companions carried him to the clubhouse where a physician administered oxygen and adrenalin, but without success.

Bing Crosby had died of a massive heart attack, aged seventy-four.

 **THE FUNERAL**

US consular officials arranged for Bing's body to be taken to the US Air Force base at Torrejon, outside Madrid. An American mortician was flown in to prepare the body for its return to the United States.

His will insisted on a private funeral. So, to avoid the expected media scrum, it began at 5 a.m. on 18 October at St Paul's Roman Catholic Church in Westwood, California. He had stipulated that only his wife and seven children should attend, but Kathryn Crosby invited Bing's siblings as well as Bob Hope, Rosemary Clooney and Phil Harris. Crosby's body lay in an open oak casket which was adorned by a single spray of red roses and his six sons acted as pall-bearers.

He was buried at the Holy Cross Cemetery, Culver City, California where his headstone reads: 'Beloved By All. Harry Lillis 'Bing' Crosby. 1904–1977', even though it is now clear that he was actually born in 1903. He is buried next to his first wife, Dixie Lee, and his parents. Neighbouring graves are occupied by Mack Sennett, Pat O'Brien, Jack Haley, Spike Jones and Jimmy Durante.

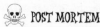 POST MORTEM

- A few hours after learning of her husband's death, Kathryn Crosby issued a statement: 'I can't think of any better way for a golfer who sings for a living to finish the round.'
- Bing Crosby was one of the wealthiest entertainers in Hollywood. He had property in Florida, as well as music holdings, and was also a part owner of the Pittsburgh Pirates baseball team. He had interests in numerous

businesses including real estate, frozen orange juice, mines, oil wells, cattle, race horses, music publishing, football and hockey teams, radio and television stations, banks, and television and film production companies. At his death he was probably worth in excess of $150 million, a huge sum of money at the time.

- Bing left money for all of his children, but there was a catch. It was left in a blind trust, until they turned sixty-five.

- Six years after his father's death, Bing's son Gary wrote a book, *Going My Own Way*, which shocked the world. Gary wrote about years of physical and emotional abuse from his father, from his nickname of 'Bucket Butt', weekly weigh-ins and beatings that drew blood. Gary wrote in the book that to help him through it all, he would dream up ways to kill his father. Gary's brother Lindsay supported the charges in the book but Bing's second family was outraged.

- Gary Crosby died of lung cancer aged sixty-two. Dennis and Lindsay both shot themselves. Phillip became a night-club owner and vehemently denied that Bing was a bad man. Nathaniel, the third of Bing's kids with his second wife Kathryn Grant, shared his father's love of golf. For several years, while still in his teens, he ran the Bing Crosby golf tournament that had been founded by his dad. In 1981 he was US Amateur champion and for three years he travelled on the European golf tour.

— ED DELAHANTY —

They say that Ed Delahanty could strike a baseball hard enough to split it in two. A leading slugger of the late nineteenth and early twentieth centuries, he is one of the few players to hit four home runs in one game and he also recorded a hitting streak of more than thirty games. His great prowess on the diamond, however, was marred by a disastrous personal life blighted by alcohol and gambling and a mental instability that would, unfortunately, prove fatal. On numerous occasions, he threatened to kill himself and his mother became so concerned about him that she would often follow him when his team went on the road, to make sure he came to no harm.

In 1900, baseball's senior league, the National League, was in turmoil. Players' wages were being reduced and teams from Washington, Baltimore, Louisville and Cleveland were dropped from the league. Byron Bancroft 'Ban' Johnson saw his opportunity and launched a rival operation, the American League, offering players better salaries and launching teams in major cities. Many of the National League's star players defected to the American League and Ed Delahanty, popularly known as Del, was seen as one of the most attractive prospects, most of the fledgling league's teams making him offers. To begin with, however, he remained loyal to his team, the Philadelphia Phillies, mainly because of a record-breaking new contract.

The following year, however, he agreed to sign for the American League's Washington Senators, receiving a $4,000 advance to do so. It was good news for the bookies, because much of that four thousand ended up in their pockets. His first year was good, however, and, aged thirty-five, and in his sixteenth season as a professional, he was the League's batting champion. Around this time, New York Giants' manager John McGraw arrived on the scene to entice Del with a huge offer – $24,000 for three seasons. He grabbed it.

He would never play for the Giants, however. An agreement between the National and American Leagues in January 1903 included the return of Delahanty to the Senators and, reluctantly, he returned to Washington. It was not a good season. His average fell and he failed to turn up for games. He was drinking heavily and on one occasion he had to be dragged from his hotel room by a team-mate after turning on the gas. He was briefly suspended and then reinstated. Then, on 25 June, the Senators travelled to Cleveland.

His drinking on this trip became monumental and his team-mates became very concerned. His behaviour became increasingly erratic – one night he drove a team-mate from his hotel room at knife-point. They headed for Detroit where his condition deteriorated still further.

On 29 June, he failed to show for the game and on the following day, he sent his wife, Norine, a telegram asking her to meet him in Washington when the Senators returned home. In a letter he also sent her he told her of an insurance policy he had taken out on himself. In the letter he expressed a macabre wish that the train would derail on the journey home – he hoped it would be 'dashed to pieces' and he along with it.

He failed to make it back to Washington, however. The day before the party was due to leave Detroit, he disappeared from the team hotel and they returned without him. However, this was not the first time Del had gone missing – six years earlier he had vanished for a week and turned up in Cincinnati.

Initially, it was thought his disappearance was a ploy to engineer a return to the Giants. Other ball-players had successfully employed this tactic. However, by 5 July the *Washington Post* was running the headline 'Where Is Delahanty?' and his family and friends were becoming concerned. Their concern was increased by a letter that arrived on 6 July. It was from a district superintendent at the railroad company informing them that Del had been thrown off a train at Fort Erie, Ontario after behaving violently towards the conductor. The letter went on to say that a man had been found by the bridge nightwatchman behaving strangely on the International Bridge that carries the railway line across the Niagara River – between Fort Erie and Buffalo. The man had reacted angrily when the nightwatchman had shone a lantern in his face and ran off. Shortly after, the nightwatchman heard a splash. The letter informed them that the man's cases had been left behind on the train and had been found to contain a Washington Senators' complementary pass, in the name of Ed Delahanty.

It later emerged that Del had been drinking whiskey heavily on the train and had begun to act wildly. He had pulled a woman from her berth by the ankles and was wielding a razor in a threatening manner. The conductor and a number of other men had ejected him from the train.

Seven days after the incident on the bridge, Ed Delahanty's body was found by a dock-worker at the *Maid of the Mist* landing stage on the Ontario side of the gorge. It had made the long journey down the Niagara River and over the Horseshoe Falls. The body had been badly mutilated during its time in the water. The stomach was split open, Del's intestines hanging out, and a propeller blade – probably belonging to the *Maid of the Mist* – had almost severed his left leg below the knee. He was wearing only a silk necktie, shoes and socks.

 THE FUNERAL

The funeral was held on 11 July at the Church of the Immaculate Conception in Cleveland and he was buried at Calvary Cemetery. His four ball-playing brothers, Jim, Frank, Joe and Tom, attended, as well as numerous friends from around the leagues. John McGraw, manager of the New York Giants, served as a pall-bearer.

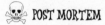 POST MORTEM

- The insurance policy had run out by the time of his death and Delahanty left his family destitute. Officials of the Senators and the American League organised benefits and donated money personally to his family.
- Norine sued the railroad company at the end of the season and was awarded an unsatisfactory $5,000.
- Ed Delahanty was inducted into baseball's Hall of Fame in 1945.

 THE CONSPIRACY THEORY

- Delahanty's family suspected foul play and the nightwatchman, Sam Kingston, came under suspicion. However, Kingston was seventy years old and it is hard to imagine him getting the better of a fit, albeit drunk, professional baseball player. However, at the time of his death, Del had been carrying a diamond ring, a diamond tie-pin, a gold watch, some other valuable trinkets as well as around $200 in cash. These had all disappeared. Strangely, Kingston had arrived home that night wearing Delahanty's hat.
- Kingston said that Del had threatened him with a piece of coal, but there was no coal on or anywhere near the bridge.
- Kingston said that he had heard Del cry for help, but he, unaccountably, took no action. He merely continued on his rounds, failing to report the incident until the next morning.

- Not long after Delahanty's body was discovered, the same dock-man at Niagara Falls found the body of a local farmer in the same place. The $1,500 he had been carrying had disappeared.

DIANA, PRINCESS OF WALES

On the morning of Saturday 30 August 1997, Diana, Princess of Wales sat enjoying the sunshine and chatting with her friend Rosa Monckton, on the deck of the *Jonkal*, the yacht owned by her boyfriend Dodi Al Fayed, which was moored off Sardinia's Emerald Coast. When breakfast arrived – coffee, croissants and jam and a groaning basket of fruit – Diana drank her usual large glass of fresh orange juice and poured hot milk in her coffee. She was relaxed, tanned and very happy after the Mediterranean idyll they had just enjoyed.

As they mused on the day ahead of them, Dodi received a call on his mobile phone from Frank Klein, president of the Ritz Hotel in Paris, owned by Dodi's father, Mohamed Al Fayed. Klein also managed the Windsor Villa, former residence of the Duke and Duchess of Windsor, which Dodi's father had been leasing from Paris city officials since 1986. Dodi informed Klein that he wanted to move into the villa, explaining that his 'friend' – if you had been reading the tabloids, you did not have to be a genius to work out who this 'friend' was – no longer wanted to live in England. 'We want to move into the villa, Frank,' said Dodi, 'because we are getting married in October or November.' The two men agreed to meet in Paris the following Monday to discuss the matter.

Having accompanied Diana back to Paris, at around 6.30 that evening Dodi went to the jewellery boutique of Alberto Repossi, to collect the $200,000 engagement ring that he had bought for Diana and which Repossi had been resizing. Although the shop was less than a hundred yards from the hotel, Dodi's obsession with security led him to insist on being driven there in his Mercedes 600. He was accompanied by Diana's bodyguard, Trevor Rees-Jones, who waited in the car while Dodi went into the shop.

Inside, he spotted another ring he thought she might like and asked Repossi if he could take both away with him to find out which the princess preferred. They returned to the hotel's Imperial Suite where Dodi decided after all on the original ring which came from a range called 'Tell Me Yes'.

Diana and Dodi had planned to eat dinner that evening at Chez Benoit, a fashionable restaurant near the Pompidou Centre. Stopping first at Dodi's ten-room apartment on the Rue Arsene-Houssaye, close to the Arc de Triomphe, they changed their minds when they spied the crowds of paparazzi waiting for them and decided instead to return to the Ritz to eat. Even there, however, the throng of tourists and photographers was so great that they could only open the car door with difficulty. A security man recalls: 'The cameras were right next to her face ... Once inside, she sat on a chair and looked ... as if she were about to cry.' Diana was distressed and Dodi was furious.

It was now almost 10 p.m. and Henri Paul, acting head of security at the Ritz, was summoned. Paul had already met the couple at the airport earlier in the day, transporting Dodi's luggage to the Arc de Triomphe apartment. He had then gone off duty at 7.05 p.m., but now rushed back to the hotel. Critically, it is not known what Paul did in the hours when he was away from the hotel. Even more critically, it is not known how much alcohol he consumed.

Back at the hotel, he was in the Vendôme bar and said by Wingfield to have been drinking 'pineapple juice, which he cut with water from a carafe, because he found it too strong'. Diana's bodyguard, Rees-Jones, later told police that Paul had been drinking a yellow liquid. That liquid turned out to be pastis.

At 11.15 Dodi announced that he had a plan to fool the paparazzi. His regular car and driver, plus a backup vehicle, would leave from the front of the hotel and act as decoys, while Diana, Dodi and Rees-Jones would drive off secretly from a rear exit with Paul at the wheel of a Mercedes S-280. In July he had employed the same scheme, but the main difference was that on that occasion his own chauffeur had been at the wheel.

After dinner, he called his father and explained his plan. Mohamed Al Fayed told him he was not happy with it, suggesting, instead, that they remain at the Ritz for the night. But Dodi refused. He had made up his mind and seemed excited.

Diana and he were later seen on the Ritz's CCTV cameras laughing and joking as they waited to make their exit.

It went wrong immediately. By the time the Mercedes stopped at traffic lights in Place de la Concorde, half a dozen photographers had caught up with it. Paul put his foot down just before the light changed and the Mercedes sped off onto the river-front expressway towards the Alma tunnel.

Disaster struck about thirty seconds later. Paul inexplicably lost control of the car and it crashed headlong, at speed, into the tunnel's thirteenth pillar. The Mercedes spun around and came to rest against the north wall, its horn blaring from the weight of Paul's dead body which had slumped over the steering wheel. He and Dodi were killed instantly and Diana and Trevor Rees-Jones, the bodyguard, were seriously injured. The impact had been so great that parts of the car's radiator were found in Paul's body.

Within seconds the paparazzi arrived and began taking pictures. The photos show Diana with blood on her forehead, but with her much-loved face unmarked. Dodi's body is on her lap and her left arm is draped over his kidskin boot.

It took fifteen minutes for the first fully equipped ambulance and its onboard doctor to arrive. Removing the princess was then a slow, delicate operation, emergency workers having to cut through metal because one of her legs was pinned under the seat. Her condition was stabilised at the scene of the crash and an ambulance then carefully drove her the 3.8 miles to hospital.

On arrival, she was still breathing, but when doctors opened her chest they found massive haemorrhaging from a torn left pulmonary vein. Doctors fought desperately to save her, repairing the wound and massaging her heart manually for two hours, but at 4 a.m. Diana, Princess of Wales, was pronounced dead at the age of thirty-six.

 THE FUNERAL

Diana's funeral took place on Saturday 6 September at Westminster Abbey amid scenes of extraordinary hysteria and sadness. Huge crowds gathered outside the Abbey and in Hyde Park, where the service was relayed on a huge screen. When her coffin emerged from Kensington Palace, borne on a gun carriage, hysterical screams rang out.

In the Abbey, Elton John sang a specially rewritten version of his song *Candle in the Wind* and Diana's brother, Earl Spencer, delivered a bold and moving eulogy that berated the paparazzi and the royal family in equal measure. 'Of all the ironies about Diana,' he said, 'perhaps the greatest is this: that a girl given the name of the ancient goddess of hunting was, in the end, the most hunted person in the modern age.' Taking a swipe at the royals who had taken away Diana's title of 'Royal Highness', he said that his sister possessed 'natural nobility ... [and] proved in the last year that she needed no royal title to continue to generate her particular blend of magic'. He vowed that his family would ensure that Diana's sons, William and Harry, were brought up 'so that their souls are not simply immersed by duty and tradition but can sing openly as [Diana] planned'. The huge crowds outside the cathedral broke into spontaneous applause. The service ended with a minute's silence that echoed around the land.

Later, as Diana's hearse made its way to her family's estate seventy-five miles away in Althorp Park, for private burial, the huge crowds lining the roadsides showered it with flowers.

The private service on an island in the middle of a lake was attended by no more than ten mourners, including Princes Charles, William and Harry.

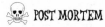 POST MORTEM

- As flowers piled high outside Kensington Palace, in the days following the princess's death, the royal family were vilified for their treatment of Diana. Eventually, the Queen calmed the situation by giving a televised speech on the Friday after the crash, speaking of her grief and her loss.
- The Queen reportedly offered to return posthumously Diana's former title of 'Her Royal Highness'. Earl Spencer rejected the offer.
- The paparazzi were initially cleared of blame by the courts. All blame was directed at the driver, Henri Paul. It was stated that he was drunk and taking antidepressants at the time of the accident. The judges determined that he had to avoid a slower-moving car as he entered the tunnel – the

elusive white Fiat Uno which, in spite of police investigating more than four thousand owners of Fiat Unos, has never been found.

- In the four weeks after the funeral, a report by the Oxford Centre for Suicide Research found that the overall suicide rate in England and Wales rose by seventeen per cent.

- The 'Tell Me Yes' ring was later found in Dodi's apartment, still in its unopened box. It now lies in a safety-deposit box in a Swiss bank, along with several love letters from Diana to Dodi.

- The 2008 inquest into the deaths of Diana and Dodi was sensational and hugely expensive. The jury ruled that the couple were killed unlawfully due to the actions of driver Henri Paul and the paparazzi. The inquest found that Paul was well over the French drink-drive limit; Diana was not pregnant; the white Fiat Uno did, indeed, exist and Diana and Dodi's car struck it a glancing blow; the three who died in the car were not wearing seatbelts; there was no plot by Prince Philip and/or MI6 to kill Diana despite evidence by Dodi's father, Mohamed Al Fayed, in which he described Prince Philip as a 'Nazi' and a 'racist', the Royal Family as 'that Dracula family' and Camilla Parker-Bowles, Prince Charles's wife, as a 'crocodile wife'; Diana did fear for her life – Lord Mishcon, Diana's lawyer, told of a conversation with her in which she claimed that the Queen was going to abdicate in favour of her son, Charles, and that she was to be sidelined by a car accident.

THE CONSPIRACY THEORY

- In his book *A Royal Duty*, Diana's former butler Paul Burrell published a handwritten letter in which Diana claimed someone was planning to kill her in a car accident by tampering with her brakes.

- There were twenty-eight errors in Henri Paul's post mortem, and no investigation into a suspiciously high carbon monoxide reading in his blood.

- It is claimed that the crime scene was not properly preserved; that the Mercedes was removed from the tunnel with 'indecent haste'; and that initially the French police were either ignorant or lied about a collision with a second car, the mysterious Fiat Uno.

- There are serious unanswered questions, some claim. These include why it took medical rescuers nearly two hours to get the Princess to a hospital; why French authorities have not made available tapes from surveillance cameras outside the Ministry of Justice (next door to the Ritz) and along the Mercedes' route; and why the British intelligence service has failed to come forth with what they know about the crash. Investigators were said to have examined enlarged stills taken from the Ritz security videotapes to identify suspicious men outside the hotel, apparently neither photographers nor tourists, shortly before Dodi and Diana fled from the rear.

- Conspiracy theorists speculate that a motorcycle worked with the Fiat Uno, pursuing the Mercedes doggedly from the Place de la Concorde, forcing it to drive faster as it approached the tunnel. There definitely was a motorcycle right behind the Mercedes, and it does not appear to have been driven by a photographer. Three witnesses, all of whom were in the eastbound lanes, described seeing a large motorcycle in the westbound lanes slow down and pass the wreck just moments after the crash.

- Suspects in Diana's death are listed variously as:
  - The Royal Family, who with the aid of British Secret Service and Parliament, and perhaps the CIA and FBI, conspired to deny a Semitic foothold to the throne. This was exacerbated by the claim that Diana was already pregnant with Dodi's child. Also, the government had been growing tired of Diana's security expenses.
  - The Pope, who recognised that the impending union of British and Arab interests threatened the security of the Vatican hegemony. This would have meant a fundamental shift in the balance of power.
  - International arms merchants who had begun to feel the financial bite of Diana's campaign against the use of landmines.
  - Diana herself, who, distressed by the possibility of a second divorce and wanting to possess Dodi forever, arranged the romantic tragedy.
  - Diana and Dodi, who faked their deaths, and in a twist of perfect irony, sold photos of their 'accident' to the tabloids for millions. They now live in quiet retirement on an island, finally free of the paparazzi who plagued them.

— CHARLES DICKENS —

In the summer of 1870, Charles Dickens was at his home, Gads Hill, near Rochester, working on his last and ultimately unfinished work, *The Mystery of Edwin Drood*. On Monday 6 June he walked his dogs into Rochester to buy a copy of the *Daily Mail*. One of his daughters, Katie, was visiting Gads Hill and was taking his other daughter, Mamie, back to London with her that day for a short visit. As they were leaving, Katie went to take her leave of her father, now back at his desk, writing after his walk. Dickens hated farewells and, normally, when he was working, would merely raise a cheek to be kissed. On this occasion, however, he stood up, took her in his arms and said 'God bless you, Katie.' She never saw him alive again.

That afternoon, Dickens rode into the village of Cobham with his sister, choosing to walk home through the park. Then, after dinner, he spent the evening in the sitting room, looking at some Chinese lanterns, bought that day, which were now lit in the conservatory. He chatted to his sister about how much he loved Gad's Hill, how he wanted his name to be forever associated with the place and how he wanted to be buried nearby.

Next morning, Dickens awoke in good spirits. He intended to work on *Edwin Drood* all day and his morning was spent in the chalet where he worked. He returned to the house for lunch and, afterwards, smoked a cigar in the conservatory before returning once more to the chalet.

Before dinner, he seemed to his sister to be tired, silent and somewhat abstracted. However, he was often like this when he had been working hard. While waiting for dinner, he wrote some letters in the library and dealt with some business matters related to meetings he was to have in London the following morning. He planned to travel there later that night.

When they sat down to dinner, his sister was shocked at how pale he looked. She asked him if he was ill and he replied that he had not felt well for about an hour. However, he would not let her send for the doctor and insisted on carrying on with dinner. He also insisted that he would still be travelling to London later.

Dickens was, in fact, having a stroke and though he fought hard against it, continuing the conversation, his speech became incoherent and indistinct. He was obviously ill and his sister begged him to go to his room while she summoned help. 'Come and lie down,' she pleaded. 'Yes, on the ground,' he replied before falling to the floor. It was a few minutes after six and those were the last words he uttered.

A couch was brought in on which he was laid and a messenger was sent to fetch the local doctor. Telegrams were sent to his family and his daughters were summoned. They arrived later that night and kept watch by his bedside. His feet were chilled and hot bricks were placed by them, but Dickens never moved and he never opened his eyes again.

On the afternoon of 9 June, the celebrated London physician Dr Russell Reynolds arrived, but could only confirm the verdict of the two doctors already in attendance, that there was no hope for the great writer. That evening, at ten past six, Dickens' daughter said that as she watched, she saw 'a shudder pass over our father, he heaved a deep sigh, a large tear rolled down his face and at that instant his spirit left us'.

 ## THE FUNERAL

Dickens had wanted to be buried in the churchyard at Shorne, but the Dean and Chapter of Rochester Cathedral requested that he be buried there. When that had been arranged, another request came that the writer's last resting place should be in Westminster Abbey. His daughters asked only that a clause in Dickens' will should be adhered to: 'I emphatically direct that I be buried in an inexpensive, unostentatious and strictly private manner.'

And so it was that on 14 June 1870, Charles Dickens, writer of *Oliver Twist*, *David Copperfield* and *Great Expectations* was buried in Westminster Abbey with just a few friends and family present.

Hundreds of people visited the grave in the weeks after his death and flowers continued to be sent, both from Britain and overseas, for many years.

- Dickens' last novel, *The Mystery of Edwin Drood*, remained unfinished at his death.
- There have been at least 180 films and television adaptations of Dickens' works, the first being a 1913 silent film version of *The Pickwick Papers*.
- A number of Dickens' characters' names and expressions have entered the dictionary. 'Gamp' is the word for 'a large, untidy, rolled-up umbrella' (Chambers Dictionary, tenth edition) and is borrowed from Mrs Sarah Gamp, a character in *Martin Chuzzlewit* who often carried an umbrella. 'Pickwickian' (resembling Mr Pickwick from *The Pickwick Papers* – round and portly) and 'Pecksniffian' (like the sanctimonious hypocritic Pecksniff in *Martin Chuzzlewit*) can also be found.
- Charles Dickens and a scene from *The Pickwick Papers* appeared on the Series E £10 note issued in Britain between 1992 and 2003.
- Dickens' eighth child, Henry Fielding Dickens, went on to become a very successful lawyer and was knighted in 1922.

— JOHN DILLINGER —

Manhattan Melodrama is a gangster film made on a modest budget about the relationship between two childhood friends, one of whom grows up to be a gangster, the other a district attorney. The movie was moderately successful on its release in 1934, but was notable for several reasons. It starred Clark Gable, about to receive his only Best Actor Oscar for his previous film, *It Happened One Night*, and it featured the first of fourteen screen pairings for the bankable duo William Powell and Myrna Loy. It was also the last film watched by the notorious bank robber John Herbert Dillinger. As he left the Biograph movie theatre in Chicago, he was ruthlessly gunned down by waiting FBI agents.

In the early 1930s, Dillinger had captured the imagination of the American public. At the time banks were low in public esteem. The Depression had forced many out of business taking with them people's life savings and they were foreclosing on businesses and homes as the economy continued to falter. Therefore, anyone getting one over on them was guaranteed to achieve a level of popularity. John Dillinger and his gang of ruthless killers did just that. Accompanied by men such as the psychopath Baby Face Nelson, Dillinger became idolised as he carried out swashbuckling bank raids and daring prison breaks across America.

He and the two gangs with which he was associated over the years stole around $300,000, about $5 million in today's terms.

For his troubles, Dillinger went to prison a number of times but he always managed to break out, in 1934 escaping from Crown Point prison in Indiana – supposedly escape-proof and guarded by large numbers of police officers and national guards-men – using a gun fashioned out of soap or wood, depending on who you listen to, and blackened with shoe polish.

However, it was this incident that would lead to Dillinger's demise. Driving over the Indiana–Illinois state line in a stolen car, he finally placed himself firmly in the jurisdiction of Herbert Hoover's fledgling FBI, created specifically to deal with the menace of 'public enemies' such as Dillinger.

The bank robberies resumed and the gang had a narrow escape while they were hiding in Wisconsin. Even surrounded by FBI agents, however, and with a reward of $20,000 on Dillinger's head, they managed to escape.

In summer 1934, Dillinger vanished. When police found his car in a side street in Chicago, they surmised he was at large in the city. He was actually in Chicago going under the assumed name of Jimmy Lawrence. Working as a clerk, he was living a fairly anonymous existence and dating a girl called Polly Hamilton.

Sunday 22 July 1934 was boiling hot, almost a hundred degrees. Word had come to the Feds that Dillinger would be going to see a movie that afternoon, in the company of two women, Polly Hamilton and Anna Sage. Sage was a Romanian brothel-keeper, original surname Cumpanas, who was under threat of deportation back to her native country. Unknown to Dillinger, she had done a deal with the authorities – she would give them Dillinger if they would lift the deportation order. She informed them of his movements that Sunday.

Manhattan Melodrama was showing at the Biograph Theater in Chicago's Lincoln Park area and the three were spotted entering the theatre, Dillinger paying. Outside waited around twenty G-Men, led by the head of the Chicago FBI office, Melvin Purgis. The plan was for Purgis to light a cigar when he saw Dillinger and the women leave the Biograph. That would be the signal for the start of the operation.

Purgis was nervous and aroused suspicions from the woman in the ticket booth as he repeatedly checked the exit during the two hours and four minutes of the performance. She informed the theatre manager who, fearing a robbery, called the police. When they arrived a few minutes later, Purgis sent them packing, flashing his badge and informing them that a stakeout was in progress.

At the appointed time, Dillinger emerged from the theatre, strolling casually between the two women. Purvis gave his signal and as he lit the cigar, Dillinger glanced at him, but suspected nothing. Agents swiftly moved in, surrounding the gangster as Purgis called out in a nervous voice: 'Stick 'em up, Johnnie. We have you surrounded.'

Dillinger instinctively reached for the gun that was secreted in the pocket of his trousers – it had been too hot to wear a jacket – but it was too late. He fell to the ground in a hail of bullets in an alley beside the theatre. Two bullets had grazed his face, close to his left eye. A third bullet hit his left clavicle and exited through the left side of his body. The fourth bullet – the one that killed him – entered the base of his neck, travelling upwards and exiting close to his right eye. He died without saying a word, aged thirty-one years and one month.

 ## THE FUNERAL

John Dillinger's body was taken to Alexian Brothers Hospital where it lay on the lawn until he was declared dead by the deputy coroner. The corpse was then transported to Cook County Morgue.

On Tuesday 24 July, Dillinger's father and half-brother travelled with a hearse containing the body across the Indiana border to the Harvey Funeral Home in Mooresville. The authorities provided a police escort – perhaps they thought Dillinger had one more audacious escape up his sleeve.

The casket was taken to the home of Dillinger's sister, Audrey Dillinger Hancock, in Maywood, Indiana, where it was put on show in her living room for about an hour, people crowding into the house to see it. Meanwhile, large throngs of curious people brought the neighbourhood to a standstill. Police became so concerned at the size of the crowds that they persuaded the Dillinger family to hold the funeral as quickly as possible.

On Wednesday 25 July John Dillinger was laid to rest during a raging thunderstorm in Crown Hill Cemetery in Indianapolis. The grave had a police guard to prevent the theft of the body until a few days later, when the grave was re-opened and concrete, mixed with chicken wire and scrap iron was poured on top of the coffin.

This was one prison John Dillinger would not be escaping from.

 ## POST MORTEM

- The souvenir-hunters had already struck by the time Dillinger's body arrived at the morgue. His clothes were already gone and a large ring he had been wearing had disappeared from his finger. In the alley, people had dipped their handkerchiefs in Dillinger's blood, creating gruesome keepsakes. Others had had more mercenary aims. There was only $7.70 in his pockets when he died, but it was claimed that he habitually carried thousands of dollars on him. It has been suggested that a police officer called Zarkovich, who had been close to Anna Sage, removed the cash from the body.
- Crowds swarmed to the Cook County Morgue where the

autopsy was carried out. The post-mortem room was thronging with doctors, nurses, police officers and FBI agents, newspapermen, society people, politicians and many others. Hundreds more gathered outside. Dillinger lay on the slab, wrapped in a winding sheet as they filed past him, women screaming and shrieking as they looked at his wounded face. Fifteen thousand people are said to have viewed the body.

- When the body arrived at Audrey's house, she was initially not convinced that it was her brother – he had had rudimentary plastic surgery carried out sometime before his death. A scar on the back of his thigh was enough to convince her, however.

- In agreement with the FBI, Anna Sage had worn an orange outfit on the day of the shooting, so that she would be recognised. Under the lights of the cinema, it had looked red and she became known as 'the Lady in Red'. She would claim she did not know the man she was with was John Dillinger. The authorities failed to hold to their end of the bargain with her and in 1936 she was deported back to Romania where she lived until her death in 1947.

- Polly Hamilton worked as a waitress in Chicago and died in 1969. A month earlier, Evelyn 'Billie' Frenchette, another of Dillinger's girlfriends, had also died. She had travelled with a crime-does-not pay carnival show when she had been released from prison.

- A third of the entire FBI budget for 1934 was used to bring down John Dillinger.

- Dillinger gang-member Baby Face Nelson was shot dead by the FBI on 27 November that same year. Another infamous member of the gang, Homer Van Meter, had died in a shoot-out with St Paul police a month after Dillinger's killing.
- It was said, although never substantiated, that John Dillinger had an unusually large penis and that J. Edgar Hoover kept it in a jar. Hoover did keep several mementoes of Dillinger – his hat, spectacles and change from his pocket – which he would proudly show off to visitors.
- 'John Dillinger Day' is celebrated by the John Dillinger Died For You Society every year on 22 July. They gather at the Biograph Theater and walk to the spot where he died, led by a bagpiper playing *Amazing Grace*.

THE CONSPIRACY THEORY

Encouraged by the fact that, on seeing the body, Dillinger's father shouted out: 'That's not my boy!' some people believed that it was not John Dillinger who died that evening. Many say that Hoover needed it to be Dillinger to save his job following several PR disasters.

There were said to be several inconsistencies:

- The body was said to have brown eyes; Dillinger's were grey.
- The Colt pistol Dillinger was supposed to have been carrying at his death and which was put on display at FBI headquarters, was actually manufactured five months *after*

the gangster's death. If this is true, some claim, Dillinger was unarmed when he was shot.

In 1963, a letter arrived at the *Indianapolis Star* containing a photograph of a man who looked like an older Dillinger, suggesting he was still alive and living anonymously.

— EDWARD II —

Edward II was never what you could call the most energetic of rulers. Son of Edward I and Eleanor of Castille, he was the first Prince of Wales and married Isabella, daughter of Philip IV of France. But his interest in the opposite sex was negligible. He was far more interested in having a good time and over-indulged in everything – food, drink and, especially, the male favourites with whom he surrounded himself. He achieved the singular position of being detested by his barons and his people in equal measure.

Attempting to engage with an English king's customary passion for subduing the Scots, Edward was ignominiously defeated by Robert the Bruce at Bannockburn in 1314 and this was followed by risings in Ireland and Wales, eroding his authority still further.

He made a truce with Scotland for thirteen years, but Charles IV of France, his wife's brother, seized his French territories. Edward sent his wife to negotiate with the French, but she hated her husband and his cronies as much as everyone else and, anyway, by this time she was having an affair with the disaffected noble Roger de Mortimer. Thus, in 1326, Isabella returned to England, landing on the Suffolk coast with a large band of Edward's enemies.

Within a month of Isabella's landfall, Edward's government had collapsed. He fled the country only to be taken prisoner on 16 November 1326, in south Wales. From there he was taken to Kenilworth Castle and his young son, Edward III, replaced him on the throne, although Isabella and Roger de Mortimer were pulling the strings.

Having been moved to Berkeley Castle, there were several attempts to free Edward. In July 1327, one of these attempts succeeded but he was recaptured just over a month later and returned to Berkeley. Eventually, Mortimer had had enough and ordered the death of the former king.

A set of chronicles known as *The Brut* tells us that:

> when that night the king had gone to bed and was asleep, the traitors, against their homage and their fealty, went quietly into his chamber and laid a large table on his stomach and with other men's help pressed him down. At this he woke and in fear of his life, turned himself upside down. The tyrants, false traitors, then took a horn and put it into his fundament as deep as they could, and took a pit of burning copper, and put it through the horn into his body, and oftentimes rolled therewith his bowels, and so they killed their lord and nothing was perceived.

In other words, Edward II died the ignominious and horrific death of having red-hot molten copper poured into his rectum.

 ## THE FUNERAL

Edward's body was placed in one coffin of lead inside another of wood and buried not at Westminster Abbey, traditional resting place of kings, but at Gloucester Cathedral.

 ## POST MORTEM

Sir Thomas Gourney and William Ogle were accused of Edward's murder but they escaped. There is no record of what became of Ogle, but Gourney was detained in Spain and is believed to have died while being brought back to England.

 ## THE CONSPIRACY THEORY

- Edward's half brother, Edmund of Woodstock, believed that Edward was not killed and was, instead, being held at Corfe Castle. Apparently, this was the result of a campaign of disinformation by agents of Roger de Mortimer seeking to entrap him (successfully as it turned out).

- Everyone seemed quite content to believe that Edward had, indeed, died until the publication of the Fieschi letter or the *Confession of Edward II* in 1878. This consisted of a letter written by a Manuele de Fieschi, Bishop of Vicelli in Italy, to Edward III. Unknown for centuries, it was discovered by a Frenchman named Alexandre Germain as he was trawling through some ecclesiastical archives. The Fieschi letter claimed that Edward II was transferred from Berkeley Castle to Corfe Castle where he was held for eighteen months before crossing into Ireland, where he remained for the next nine months. Then, disguised as a hermit, he returned to England and sailed to the Continent, travelling across France to Avignon where he was received by the Pope. After further travels he settled in Milan which is where he came to the attention of Manuele de Fieschi.

ARCHDUKE FRANZ FERDINAND

Gavrilo Princip was born in Bosnia-Herzegovina in 1894. The son of a postman, he had eight siblings, six of them dying in infancy, and from an early age he suffered from tuberculosis. In 1912, Princip travelled to Belgrade to continue his education and, in Serbia, joined the secret nationalist organisation the Black Hand Society. For the next two years most of his spare time was spent with other nationalists who favoured a union between Bosnia-Herzegovina and Serbia and independence from the Austro-Hungarian Empire.

It was announced that Archduke Franz Ferdinand, the heir to the throne of the Austro-Hungarian Empire, was going to visit Bosnia-Herzegovina in June 1914 and tour the capital on the anniversary of the 1389 battle of Kosovo, a humiliating collective memory for all Serbs, in which Serbia was defeated by the Turks, ending Serbia's independence as a nation. In response to the announcement, Dragutin Dimitrijević, the chief of the Intelligence Department in the Serbian Army and head of the Black Hand, sent a number of men, including Princip, to Sarajevo to assassinate the Archduke.

Dimitrijević also considered Franz Ferdinand a serious threat to a union between Bosnia-Herzegovina and Serbia. He was worried that Ferdinand's plans to grant concessions to the South Slavs would make an independent Serbian state more difficult to achieve.

The assassins were each given a revolver, two bombs and a small vial of cyanide. Like modern-day suicide bombers, they were to kill themselves after they had killed the Archduke. Dimitrijević was, of course, especially keen that no one would be left alive to say who was behind the assassination.

Word got out about the plot, however, and Nikola Pašić, Prime Minister of Serbia, fearing that an assassination would lead to war with Austria-Hungary, issued orders for the men's arrest when they left the country. The orders were never implemented, however.

On Sunday 28 June Franz Ferdinand and his pregnant wife, Princess Sophie von Chotkovato, arrived by train at Sarajevo station, from where they were taken to the City Hall for a reception hosted by General Oskar Potiorek, governor of Bosnia-Herzegovina. The Mayor of Sarajevo and the city's Commissioner of Police rode in the first car and in the second, the top rolled back to let the crowd see the royal couple, were the Archduke and his wife, accompanied by Potiorek and Count von Harrach.

The members of the Black Hand group spaced themselves out along the route, each with orders to take action as the car passed.

Muhamed Mehmedbašić was the first to see the car but he took fright and the motorcade passed unharmed. He later claimed that there had been a policeman nearby and he feared he would be arrested before he had a chance to throw his bomb.

Nedjelko Čabrinović was next and he held his nerve, stepping out of the crowd at 10.15 a.m. and launching his bomb at the royal car. Seeing the bomb, Sophie ducked and Franz Ferdinand deflected it with his arm, causing it to bounce off the back of the vehicle and explode under the car behind them, seriously injuring Eric von Merizzi and Count Boos-Waldeck, two of the car's occupants, as well as a number of spectators. Franz Urban, the Archduke's driver, accelerated and the Archduke's car sped through the streets of Sarajevo to City Hall, making it impossible for any of the other conspirators to carry out their plans.

Following his orders to the letter, Čabrinović swallowed his cyanide and jumped into the River Miljacka, pursued by several men, including two detectives. Unfortunately for him, however, the poison did not work and he was apprehended and taken to the nearest police station.

In spite of all this, the reception went ahead as planned and when it was over Franz Ferdinand insisted on being taken to the hospital to visit those who had been injured in the attack. When it was suggested that this might be dangerous, Oskar Potiorek replied: 'Do you think Sarajevo is full of assassins?'

Nevertheless, Potiorek *did* conclude that the city centre

might be dangerous and devised a route straight along the Appel Quay to the hospital. Unfortunately, he forgot to tell Franz Urban and the royal driver turned right into Franz Joseph Street where Gavrilo Princip just happened to be standing on the corner. Realising that the driver had taken a wrong turn, Potiorek shouted at him. Urban stopped the car and began to reverse, moving slowly past Princip who stepped forward, drew his gun and, from a distance of about two metres, fired several shots into the car, hitting the Archduke in the neck and Sophie in the abdomen.

Franz Ferdinand had been hit in the jugular vein and as Count von Harrach, travelling in the car with them, took out his handkerchief to wipe away the blood from the Archduke's lips Sophie cried out: 'For God's sake! What happened to you?' Then she sank down with her face between the Archduke's knees. She had fainted from shock. The Archduke exclaimed, 'Sophie, Sophie, don't die. Live for my children.'

Von Harrach seized the Archduke by the coat collar to prevent his head from sinking forward and asked him if he was in great pain. Franz Ferdinand clearly answered 'It is nothing,' his face slightly distorted. He then repeated this six or seven times, every time drifting closer to unconsciousness as his voice faded. Then there was a brief pause followed by a convulsive rattle in his throat.

The car sped off to the governor's residence at Konak, but the royal pair died soon after they arrived.

THE FUNERAL

Franz Ferdinand and Princess Sophie were given a joint funeral Mass, but her plinth was placed eighteen inches lower than his, evidence of lingering antagonism from his family towards her due to the fact that she was not a member of one of the reigning European dynasties. They were buried in the crypt of their country home, Scloss Artstetten.

POST MORTEM

- Following his orders, after shooting Franz Ferdinand and Sophie von Chotkovato, Princip turned his gun on himself, but a man behind him realised what he was doing and seized his right arm. A couple of policemen joined the struggle and Princip was arrested.
- Princip and Nedjelko Čabrinović were both interrogated by the police, eventually giving the names of their fellow conspirators. Muhamed Mehmedbašić managed to escape to Serbia but Trifko Grabez, Danilo Ilic, Vaso Cubrilovic, Cvijetko Popovic, Misko Jovanovic and Veljko Cubrilovic were arrested and charged with treason and murder.
- The eight men were found guilty. Under Austro-Hungarian law, capital punishment could not be imposed on anyone under the age of twenty. Princip, nineteen years and eleven months at the time of the assassination, consequently received the maximum penalty of twenty years.

- Princip's only sign of regret was the statement that he was sorry he had killed the wife of the Archduke. He had aimed only at her husband and would have preferred that the other bullet should have struck General Potiorek.

- Nedjelko Čabrinović's statement in court said: 'We thought that only people of noble character were capable of committing political assassinations. We heard it said that he (Archduke Franz Ferdinand) was an enemy of the Slavs. Nobody directly told us "kill him"; but in this environment, we arrived at the idea ourselves. I would like to add something else. Although Princip is playing the hero, and although we all wanted to appear as heroes, we still have profound regrets. In the first place, we did not know that the late Franz Ferdinand was a father. We were greatly touched by the words he addressed to his wife: "Sophie, stay alive for our children." We are anything you want, except criminals. In my name and in the name of my comrades, I ask the children of the late successor to the throne to forgive us. As for you, punish us according to your understanding. We are not criminals. We are honest people, animated by noble sentiments; we are idealists; we wanted to do good; we have loved our people; and we shall die for our ideals.'

- Austrian reaction to the assassination was swift, as the Sarajevo crisis was seen as the Empire's last chance to assert its supremacy in the Balkans. Austrian foreign minister Count Leopold von Berchtold was determined to make use of the assassinations to crush once and for all the Serbian nationalist movement. He sent an envoy to Berlin, who was assured by Emperor William II that Germany would fully support any action the Dual Monarchy might take against Serbia. On 6 July, German Chancellor Theobald von Bethmann-Hollweg issued the blank cheque of unconditional German support.

- On 23 July 1914, Austria-Hungary presented Serbia with a lengthy list of demands, with a forty-eight-hour period in which to comply. These demands included abolishing all pan-Serb propaganda, expelling from office any persons thought to have nationalist sympathies, taking legal action against certain officials designated by Austria-Hungary, and allowing agents of the Dual Monarchy to control all investigations and proceedings concerning the Sarajevo murders. Minutes before the 25 July deadline, Serbia issued a conciliatory reply to von Berchtold's demands, stating that Serbia wished the dispute to be submitted to the International Tribunal at The Hague. This conciliation was rejected. On 28 July 1914, Austria-Hungary declared war on Serbia. World War I had begun.

- Gavrilo Princip's tuberculosis finally killed him on 28 April 1918, shortly before the end of the war his actions had precipitated.

— F. SCOTT FITZGERALD —

Scott Fitzgerald had been an alcoholic since college. Although he wrote sober and claimed only to be a social drinker, he was known to bribe waiters to bring him glasses of straight gin, masquerading as water. In addition to his alcoholism, he had suffered from tuberculosis on and off since 1919, enduring a tubercular haemorrhage in 1929, and was a victim of depression resulting from his guilt over the incarceration of his wife, Zelda, in a succession of hospitals and asylums.

The golden years of the Jazz Age, of which Fitzgerald was the acknowledged chronicler, had long passed. In 1920, aged twenty-four, he had achieved fame with the publication of his first novel, *This Side of Paradise*, but he and Zelda, who he married shortly after the book's publication, lived opulently, consistently spending more than they earned. Fitzgerald was forced to write short stories for magazines such as *The Saturday Evening Post*, *Collier's Weekly* and *Esquire*. But even with the income from these and the sale of movie rights for his books and short stories, he was continually borrowing from his agent, Harold Ober, and his faithful editor at Scribner's,

Maxwell Perkins, to pay Zelda's medical bills and maintain his exuberant lifestyle.

Following a period of relentless financial stress, drunkenness and depression in the mid 1930s, described by him in his essay *The Crack-Up*, he found some relief, financially, at least, in Hollywood, working on further commercial short stories and earning $1,000 a week writing scripts for Metro-Goldwyn-Mayer. He also started his fifth and final novel, the ultimately unfinished *The Love of the Last Tycoon*, based on the life of film mogul Irving Thalberg.

His personal life also improved. Estranged from Zelda, who would spend the rest of her life in institutions, he began a relationship with the nationally syndicated gossip columnist, English-born Sheila Graham. Graham had been engaged to the Marquess of Donegall, but had broken off the engagement within a month of meeting Fitzgerald.

Meanwhile, his health continued to deteriorate, leading to a stay in hospital in 1939, ostensibly for treatment for tuberculosis. It has been speculated, however, that he was actually being treated for his drinking.

Towards the end of November 1940, Fitzgerald had a serious heart attack in Schwab's Drug Store on Sunset Boulevard – an important meeting place for people in the movie industry. To aid his recovery, his doctor recommended he avoid strenuous exertion and suggested that he find an apartment on the ground floor to avoid stairs. Sheila Graham conveniently lived in a ground-floor apartment and he moved in with her.

Fitzgerald was worried enough to stop drinking and took to his bed to work on *The Love of the Last Tycoon*.

On the night of 20 December he suffered a second heart attack and the next day, Sheila Graham found him on the floor of their living room. He had suffered a third and fatal heart attack as he awaited a visit from his doctor.

He was forty-four.

 THE FUNERAL

When she arrived at a memorial service at the Hollywood funeral home in which Fitzgerald's body was kept before his funeral, writer Dorothy Chandler uttered: 'The poor son of a bitch,' a line spoken in *The Great Gatsby* by the philosopher Owl Eyes, during a eulogy at the funeral of Jay Gatsby.

Fitzgerald's body was shipped to Rockville, Maryland, where Saint Mary's Catholic Church refused to allow him to be interred in the family plot because he had been a non-practising Catholic at the time of his death. Consequently, he was buried at Rockville Union Cemetery in a funeral attended by only a handful of people.

In 1975, after a campaign waged by Scott and Zelda's daughter, Scottie, the bodies of both Scott and Zelda were moved to Saint Mary's Church.

Their tombstone bears the final words of *The Great Gatsby*: 'So we beat on, boats against the current, borne back ceaselessly into the past.'

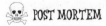

- At the time of his death, none of Fitzgerald's books was in print. *The Love of the Last Tycoon* – originally known as *The Last Tycoon* – remained only half written. It was edited by his friend Edmund Wilson and published in 1941 as *The Last Tycoon*. Despite being unfinished, it is regarded as a master-piece.

- Fitzgerald's heart condition cannot have been helped by his love of all things sweet – he loved Coca Cola, poured huge amounts of sugar into his coffee and was practically addicted to fudge.

- At his death, Fitzgerald's life and career were considered a warning to aspiring writers. In the opinion of most critics, he had failed to fulfil his genius. Typical of the reviews of his work was a headline over a review of *The Great Gatsby* when it was first published – 'F. Scott Fitzgerald's Latest Dud'.

- The author Nathaniel West and his wife, Eileen McKenney, were killed in a car accident in El Centro, California, en route to Fitzgerald's memorial service in Los Angeles. Although it was common knowledge that West was an awful driver and many of his friends refused to get into a car with him, it is suggested that he was so grief-stricken by the death of his close friend that he drove through a red light.

- Zelda began writing an unfinished novel of her own, *Caesar's Things*, after reading *The Love of the Last Tycoon*. She did not attend Fitzgerald's funeral and spent the next five years checking in and out of Highland Hospital in Ashville, North Carolina, where Fitzgerald had placed her in 1936. Her schizophrenia did not respond to treatment and on the night of 10 March 1948, she was one of nine women killed in a fire at the hospital.

- After the 1950s, Fitzgerald's oeuvre underwent a reappraisal. By 1960, *The Great Gatsby* was being recognised as the Great American novel and Fitzgerald himself was acknowledged to be one of America's greatest-ever writers.

— MAHATMA GANDHI —

On Friday 30 January 1948, seventy-eight-year-old Mahatma Gandhi woke punctually, as always, at half past three in the morning. It was just twelve days since his successful fast to bring about a rapprochement between Hindus and Muslims in Delhi. But ten days previously there had been an attempt on his life when a bomb exploded a short distance from where he was addressing a prayer meeting. As he opened his eyes that morning, he knew his life was in danger.

Rising from the wooden plank on which he slept, Gandhi woke his grand-nieces, Manu and Abha, and assistant, Brij Krishna Chandiwala. They said prayers and then Manu and Abha, whom he called his walking sticks, helped him walk into the inner room where his legs were covered with a blanket. The sun had not yet risen as he worked on the draft of a proposal for a new constitution for his party, Congress, written the previous night for the forthcoming Congress Working Committee meeting. It would become known as Gandhi's Last Will and Testament to the nation. At 4.45 he drank a glass of lemon, honey and hot water and, one hour later, his daily glass of orange juice.

Gandhi was still very weak from his fast and, already tired, he slept for thirty minutes. Following that, he had his first meeting of the day while taking his morning constitutional, walking around his room. He left to have a massage, handing his draft for the new constitution to his secretary, Pyarelal, and asking him to have a look at it and fill in any gaps he might find.

Brij Krishna gave Gandhi a half-hour massage in a room next door to his sitting room, with two electric heaters warming the cold morning air, and as he lay on the table, the Mahatma read the morning papers. Manu then gave him his bath following which he was weighed. He weighed 109.5 pounds and had put on 2.5 pounds since ending the fast.

At 9.30, Gandhi had his breakfast – cooked vegetables, twelve ounces of goat's milk, four tomatoes, four oranges, carrot juice and a decoction of ginger, sour limes and aloes. He talked with his secretary and told him that he planned to go to Pakistan. An old friend from his South African days, Rustom Sorabji, then paid a visit with his family.

At 10.30, Gandhi again slept and the soles of his feet were rubbed with ghee. Waking at midday, he drank some hot water and honey and then walked unaided to the bathroom, the first time since his fast that he had done so.

He welcomed a delegation of Delhi Muslim leaders and after more meetings, he lay down in the sunshine and had an abdominal mud pack applied, wearing a peasant's bamboo hat while Kanu and Abha again massaged his feet. When told that the papers claimed that he was leaving for Sevagram, his ashram, on 1 February, Gandhi replied enigmatically: 'Yes, the papers have announced that Gandhi would be going on the first, but who that Gandhi is, I do not know.'

At around 1.30, he drank a few ounces of carrot and lemon juice and met some blind and homeless refugees. Then, at 2.15, the daily round of interviews began with some of the journalists and broadcasters from India and beyond who constantly sought audiences with the great man. He did not finish his last interview until 4 p.m.

Another meeting followed and as he talked, Gandhi ate his evening meal – goat's milk, vegetable soup, oranges and carrot juice. He then asked for his charka – spinning wheel. The spinning wheel was a powerful symbol for Gandhi. For him it represented a technology which was simple and could be used by everyone.

The customary time for prayers was 5 p.m., but Gandhi was already ten minutes late on this occasion, having forgotten to put on the Ingersoll watch he normally wore. He was told the time and reluctantly got up, put on his sandals – and went through the side door out into the twilight. He was wearing a shawl and was leaning on Manu on his right and Abha on his left. Manu carried his spittoon, glasses case and rosary as well as her notebook. Brij Krishna walked behind them with members of the Birla family, the owners of the house, and some others.

Since the failed assassination attempt a few weeks previously, about thirty policemen, uniformed and plain clothes, were stationed around Birla House, but today the Mahatma's personal plain-clothes policeman was absent, having been re-assigned elsewhere.

As he was late, Gandhi did not follow his usual route through the leafy arbour to the right side of the grounds. Instead, he took a short cut across the lawn to the steps that led to the terrace where prayers were held. His mood was light. He joked about the raw carrot Abha had given him that day, calling it cattle food. She replied that Ba, Gandhi's deceased wife, used to call it horse food. As they hurried along, Gandhi replied: 'Is it not grand of me to relish what no one else would care for?'

At the top of the steps, the Mahatma brought his palms together in greeting. The hushed crowd, several hundred strong, parted to make a passage for him to the wooden plat-form. Critically, no one walked in front of Gandhi.

The Mahatma had taken just a few paces from the steps when Nathuram Godse, a member of the right-wing political organisation the Hindu Mahasabha, whose members deeply resented what they saw as Gandhi's appeasement of India's Muslims, pushed his way through the crowd and approached Gandhi with his palms joined. A tiny, black, Italian Beretta pistol was hidden between them, easily smuggled in as Gandhi did not allow the police to search people entering the grounds of Birla House for the prayer meetings. Godse bowed low and said: 'Namaste, Gandhiji,' and Gandhi acknowledged him, joining his palms together. Manu thought Godse was going to kiss the Mahatma's feet, something that she knew the holy man did not like. So, she motioned him away. 'Brother, Bapu is already late for prayers,' she said. 'Why are you bothering him?'

Godse pushed her aside with his left hand, the gun in his right hand momentarily exposed. She dropped the glasses case and the other things she was carrying and for several moments she carried on arguing with the assailant, but when the rosary fell to the ground, she bent down to retrieve it. At this moment, Godse pulled the trigger and fired three bullets into Gandhi's abdomen and chest at almost point-blank range. Gandhi remained standing, his palms still together in greeting. Then he was heard to gasp 'He Ram, He Ram' ('Oh God, Oh God'). He slowly sank to the ground, palms still joined. The air was filled with gunsmoke and confusion and panic reigned.

The Mahatma was now slumped on the ground, his head resting in one of his horrified nieces' laps. His face had turned deathly white, his white, Australian wool shawl turning red with his blood. Within seconds Mahatma Gandhi was dead. It was 5.17 p.m.

 THE FUNERAL

On 13 February 1948, almost a million people accompanied Mahatma Gandhi's funeral procession to the cremation grounds by the holy waters of the Yamuna, near New Delhi.

A funeral pyre of stone, brick and earth had been built at

Rajghat, close to the river, eight feet square and two feet high. Long, thin sandalwood logs, sprinkled with incense, were stacked on it. The Mahatma's body was placed on it with his head to the north and at 4.45 p.m., Ramdas, Gandhi's third son, set the pyre alight, accompanied by a huge groan from the crowd. Ramdas later consigned some of the ashes to the Ganges.

Later, in similar ceremonies at sacred sites along rivers and seashores at some fifty places in India and Pakistan, portions of Gandhi's ashes were ceremoniously committed to the waters in the presence of millions of mourners. Millions more, in towns and villages with community wireless sets, listened to a three-hour commentary on the Allahabad ceremony, broadcast in English and Hindi by All-India Radio. All work throughout the country stopped that day, the last of a thirteen-day period of state mourning.

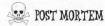 POST MORTEM

The film *Gandhi*, directed by Richard Attenborough and starring Ben Kingsley in an uncanny recreation of the Mahatma, is judged one of the greatest biopics ever made. For Gandhi's funeral which begins the film, Attenborough hoped for a mostly unpaid crowd of 150,000 people. On the day, an extra quarter of a million turned up, making it easily the biggest crowd ever to appear in a film.

─ CARY GRANT ─

In 1986, the man christened Archibald Leach, who had shot to fame as the debonair and handsome Cary Grant, was touring the United States with his show *A Conversation with Cary Grant*, a lecture with film clips and a question and answer session. On the night of Friday 28 November he arrived with his wife, Barbara Harris, at the Blackhawk Hotel in Davenport, Iowa, where he was due to do a show the following night at the Adler theatre.

On Saturday afternoon, Grant arrived at the theatre for the 4 p.m. rehearsal for the evening's 8.30 performance. According to all present, he and his wife were in very good spirits and the star looked, as ever, great. Just before the rehearsal began, the event's sponsor remarked to him 'I hope everything goes okay with the show,' to which Grant replied morosely, but in that distinctive voice, 'What happens, happens.'

Perhaps he was right to be morose because what did happen was that quite soon after he began to feel ill and vomited. He complained to his wife of a sudden and severe headache. He was taken from the stage to his dressing room in a wheelchair and after some time was eventually persuaded to return to his hotel, next door to the theatre. Ever the trouper, he resisted suggestions that a doctor be called, worrying that the performance would have to be cancelled. But his condition deteriorated and there was no option but to cancel.

Eventually two doctors were called to examine him and at 9.15 p.m., he was taken by ambulance to St Luke's Hospital. By the time the ambulance arrived at the hospital, however, he was in a coma and after forty-five minutes of tests, they rushed him into intensive care.

On duty that night was Dr James Gilson, a Davenport cardiologist, who assessed that Grant had had a massive stroke and concluded that there was little that could be done: his brain was badly damaged and he could no longer talk. One side of his body was completely paralysed and his pupils were dilated. 'Cary felt no pain,' Dr Gilson said, 'and the family were very nice throughout the ordeal, and thanked me for all that was done.'

At 11.22 p.m., Cary Grant died, aged eighty-two.

 THE FUNERAL

At 3 a.m. the following morning Barbara Harris accompanied her husband's body back to Los Angeles on a charter flight. On Sunday 30 November his body was taken to Burbank where it was cremated by the Neptune Society, an organisation founded to provide 'a simple and dignified disposition of the decedent's remains at the time of death'. In his will, Grant had stated: 'I desire that my remains be cremated, and there be no formal services to note my passing.' His ashes were handed over to his wife and Jennifer, the daughter of his marriage to actress Dyan Cannon.

POST MORTEM

After his death the questions about whether Cary Grant was gay or not arose again. To this day, they remain unanswered, although there has always been much speculation about his relationship with fellow actor Randolph Scott. The film director George Cukor, interviewed for the book *Hollywood Gays*, said: 'Oh, Cary won't talk about it. At most, he'll say they did some wonderful pictures together. But Randolph did admit it – to a friend … a male nurse … (Scott was housebound in later years). He'd shown the nurse his scrapbook on Grant, and when the nurse asked him if it was true about their relationship, Randolph just smiled and nodded.' However, Scott's son, interviewed for a BBC documentary about Cary Grant, claimed that his father and Cary never could have had an affair because his father's anus was checked when he was in the hospital, and 'you can tell'!

ERNESTO CHE GUEVARA

Che Guevara and his group of followers – consisting of Cubans, Argentineans, Peruvians and Bolivians – had been attacking the Bolivian Army with considerable success since spring 1967. At the end of August however, the army had retaliated with a significant victory, wiping out a third of his force. To make matters worse, after months of fighting, the guerrilla leader's health was beginning to fail.

Two years earlier he had suddenly resigned from his positions as president of Cuba's national bank and Minister of Industry and had said farewell to the Cuban Revolution he had created with his brother-in-arms, Fidel Castro. He wanted to export revolution to Latin America and Africa and in pursuit of this ambition, he left Cuba to set up guerrilla forces first in the Congo and then in Bolivia.

By 29 September Che and seventeen of his men were trapped in Valle Serrano, in the jungles of south-east Bolivia, and the Second Ranger Battalion of the Bolivian Army was ordered into the area to deal with them. This force of 1,300 men had been trained and equipped by US Green Berets and was being directed by the CIA, with one aim and one aim only – the capture of Che Guevara.

On 8 October in Quebrada del Yuro at around 1.30 p.m. Che's final battle began.

The army had received word that the guerrillas were located in the Churro Ravine and, on entering the area, they immediately encountered a group of them. Che and a colleague, Simeon Cuba 'Willy' Sarabia, a former Bolivian tin miner, tried to break out but a machine-gun crew caught sight of them and opened fire, hitting Che in the leg several times. He was helped by Willy in the direction of the Tuscal Ravine where the two men rested for a few minutes. They then began to move north, but it was directly into the line of fire of some government soldiers. A gunfight erupted and Che was hit again in the right leg. His gun was knocked out of his hand as another bullet pierced his right forearm. As soldiers approached, he realised it was futile and shouted, 'Don't shoot! I'm Che Guevara and I am worth more to you alive than dead.' By 3.30 the battle was over and he and Willy had been taken prisoner.

The soldier in charge of the operation, Captain Prado, immediately ordered his radio operator to signal the divisional headquarters in Vallegrande to give them the news that the famous guerrilla had at last been captured. The coded message read, 'Hello Saturno, we have Papá!' Saturno was the code for Colonel Joaquin Zenteno, commandant of the Eighth Bolivian Army Division, and Papá was code for Che. The incredulous colonel asked Prado to confirm the message before wild celebrations erupted amongst the divisional headquarters staff. Zenteno ordered Prado to immediately transfer Che and all other prisoners to the nearby village of La Higuera.

Unable to walk due to his wounds, Che was carried on a blanket by four soldiers to La Higuera, seven kilometres away, arriving there not long after dark. He and Sarabia were put into the village's one-room schoolhouse.

At 6.15 a.m., CIA operative Félix Rodríguez – later involved in the Iran/Contras scandal and nowadays a close friend of the Bush family – arrived by helicopter, along with Colonel Zenteno. Rodríguez brought a powerful portable field radio and a camera with a special four-footed stand normally used to photograph documents. He described the scene in the schoolhouse as 'gruesome'. Che was lying in dirt, his arms tied behind his back and his feet bound together, next to the bodies of the other guerrillas who had been taken. Rodríguez described him as looking 'like a piece of trash', with matted hair, torn clothes, and wearing only pieces of leather on his feet for shoes. 'I had mixed emotions when I first arrived there,' he recalled later. 'Here was the man who had assassinated many of my countrymen. And nevertheless, when I saw him, the way he looked ... I felt really sorry for him.'

Rodríguez set up his radio and transmitted a coded message to a South American CIA station that was forwarded to the CIA headquarters in Langley, United States. He also photographed Che's diary and other captured documents. Later, he spent time talking with Che and had his picture taken with him. He took the guerrilla's wristwatch as a souvenir.

By 10 a.m., the Bolivian officers were faced with the dilemma of what to do with the revolutionary. He could not be prosecuted because a trial would attract world attention and could conceivably generate sympathetic propaganda for him and for Cuba. Therefore, the decision was taken to execute him. The official story would be that he died from wounds received in battle.

Rodríguez received a call from Superior Command at Vallegrande and was ordered to conduct Operation Five Hundred and Six Hundred. Five Hundred was the Bolivian code for Che and Six Hundred was the order to kill him. He informed Colonel Zenteno of the order, but also told him that the US government had instructed *him* to keep Che alive at all costs. The CIA had arranged helicopters and planes to take him to Panama for interrogation. But Zenteno said he must obey his own orders and Rodríguez decided 'to let history take its course', as he later put it.

He went into the schoolhouse to tell Che of the orders from Bolivian high command. Che admitted: 'It is better like this ... I should never have been captured alive.' He gave Rodríguez a message for his wife and one for Castro. The two men embraced and Rodríguez left the room.

A captain by the name of Perez entered the schoolhouse and asked Che if he wanted anything before he died. Che replied that he only wanted to 'die with a full stomach'. When Perez sneeringly asked him if he was 'materialist', Che replied, as he had to most of the questions the Bolivians had asked him, 'Perhaps'. Perez called him a 'poor shit' and left.

No one amongst the non-commissioned officers was willing to volunteer to carry out the execution and they decided to draw lots. Sergeant Jaime Teran pulled the shortest one and went nervously to the schoolhouse where he found Che leaning against the wall. He asked to be allowed to stand up for his execution. 'I know what you have come for and I am ready,' he said. Teran was terrified, however, and fled the building, immediately being ordered to return by his senior officers.

When Teran entered the building, Che said he would remain standing. Teran angrily told him to sit down, but Che retorted: 'I know you have come to kill me. Shoot, you are only going to kill a man.' These were the last words Che Guevara spoke. Teran, averting his gaze from the guerrilla leader's face, shot him in the arms and legs and then in the thorax. Other soldiers came into the schoolhouse at that point and took their turn at shooting into the corpse of the legendary revolutionary.

POST MORTEM

- Following the execution, Che's body was exhibited for twenty-four hours before disappearing. The authorities were afraid of creating a place of pilgrimage for his sympathisers.
- His hands were amputated and preserved in formaldehyde as evidence that he was dead.
- Two doctors at the hospital in Vallegrande, Bolivia, signed a death certificate which stated that 'on 9 October at

5.30 p.m., there arrived ... Ernesto Guevara Lynch, approximately forty years of age, the cause of death being multiple bullet wounds in the thorax and extremities. Preservative was applied to the body.' On the same day, an autopsy report recorded the multiple bullet wounds found in Che's body. 'The cause of death,' stated the autopsy report, 'was the thorax wounds and consequent haemorrhaging.'

- On 14 October, students at the Central University of Venezuela protested at US involvement in Che's death. Demonstrations were organised against the American Embassy, American businesses and the homes of American ex-pats.

- On 15 October, Bolivian President Barrientos claimed that Che had been cremated and his ashes had been secretly buried somewhere in the Vallegrande region.

- On 16 October, the Bolivian Armed Forces released a communiqué on the death of Che Guevara. The communiqué was 'based on documents released by the Military High Command on 9 October ... concerning the combat that took place at La Higuera between units of the Armed Forces and the red group commanded by Ernesto "Che" Guevara, as a result of which he, among others, lost his life'. The report stated that Guevara died 'more or less at 8 p.m. on Sunday, October 8 ... as a result of his wounds'.

- On 18 October, Fidel Castro delivered a eulogy for Che to nearly a million people – one of his largest audiences ever – in Havana's Plaza de la Revolución. Castro proclaimed that

Che's lifelong struggle against imperialism and his ideals would be the inspiration for future generations of revolutionaries. His life was a 'glorious page of history' because of his extraordinary military accomplishments and his unequalled combination of virtues which made him an 'artist in guerrilla warfare'. Castro claimed that Che's murderers would be disappointed when they realised that 'the art to which he dedicated his life and intelligence cannot die'.

- In 1995, Mario Vargas Salinas, a soldier who had taken part in the secret burial of Che's body, said that the revolutionary and his comrades had been interred in a pit dug by a bulldozer near Vallegrande's airstrip. He was unable, however, to recall the precise location. In 1997, aerial technology was used to find areas in the earth where the ground had been disturbed. A trough was dug and human remains found. One of the skeletons had no hands and was covered by a military jacket. It was Che Guevara.

- On 13 July 1997, a ceremony in Havana, attended by Fidel Castro and other Cuban officials, marked the return of Che's remains to Cuba.

- On 17 October 1997, at a ceremony attended by Castro and thousands of Cubans, Che was reburied in Santa Clara, Cuba.

- In the small town where Che's remains were found, the people who knew the revolutionary when he was alive now talk about him not as a human, but as a 'brujo' – a sorcerer. They say it doesn't matter that his remains have been found. He is still alive in spirit form.

— GEORGE HARRISON —

George Harrison had always been a heavy smoker, the Beatles' love for 'ciggies' being well known from their earliest days. In 1997 he was diagnosed with throat cancer but succeeded in overcoming it. By 2001, he had developed lung cancer and knew that it was terminal. He contacted Gavin de Becker – the guru of celebrity security – during his stay in Staten Island University Hospital where he was registered under the name Arias while receiving last-chance cancer treatment, to arrange a secretive funeral.

Around this time, ten days before his death on 29 November 2001, he was visited by fellow ex-Beatle Paul McCartney. McCartney has described how they held hands and laughed and joked during their last few hours together.

George was adamant that he would not die in a hospital and McCartney offered his Beverley Hills mansion, formerly owned by Kurt Cobain's widow, Courtney Love. So, the dying guitarist travelled to UCLA Medical Centre for drugs and pain management before heading for Paul's house to die.

For thirty-six hours George drifted in and out of consciousness, his wife Olivia and son Dhani at his bedside.

George's old friend, the sitar-player Ravi Shankar, was present and played throughout the vigil. Pictures of the Hindu gods Krishna and Rama were placed at the bedside and two of George's friends from the Krishna faith, Shayam Sundara and Mukunda, chanted quietly in a corner.

'All things must pass,' the fifty-eight-year-old ex-Beatle once sang. In his case, it was serene.

 ## THE FUNERAL

George's body was wrapped in a shawl and covered with holy oils. An unmarked white van from Hollywood Forever Cemetery arrived to collect the body. The funeral attendants briefly joined hands with the Harrison family and the security staff, and said a small prayer. The van stopped briefly at the doctor's for the death certificate to be signed and then took him to the cemetery crematorium, where he was cremated in a cardboard casket, in a Krisnha service.

On the following Monday his ashes arrived in India where they were scattered in Allahabad where the three holiest rivers in Hinduism converge – the Ganges, the Yamuna and the Saraswati.

POST MORTEM

- The Harrison family released a statement: 'We are deeply touched by the outpouring of love and compassion from people around the world. The profound beauty of the moment of George's passing – of his awakening from this dream – was no surprise to those of us who knew how he longed to be with God. In that pursuit, he was relentless.'

- The world was invited to join Olivia and Dhani in a minute of meditation the following Monday at 1.30 p.m.

- George was survived by his brothers Harry and Peter and sister Louise as well as by his first wife, Pattie Boyd, whom he had met in 1964 on the set of the Beatles' first film, *A Hard Day's Night*.

- According to press reports and many of the obituaries, George died in the home of his friend Gavin de Becker. His death certificate describes the 'place of death' as an address in Coldwater Canyon, Beverley Hills. However, the Coldwater Canyon address is non-existent. Paul McCartney's house is accepted to be the most likely place of death. It is thought that the ex-Beatle tried to create a smokescreen so that the property in which he died could not become a stop on Hollywood's ghoulish death tours or feature in books such as this.

— BUDDY HOLLY —

It was a time of change for Buddy Holly. He had broken up his backing group, the Crickets, and had left his record company. Recently married and with a child on the way, he badly needed the money that touring provided and so had agreed to take part in *The Winter Dance Party* tour, a gruelling procession of one-night stands across the American Midwest in the middle of winter. Worse still, the tour bus was unheated and kept breaking down. It was so bad that drummer Carl Brunch suffered from frostbite.

Headlining the tour were Holly, Richie Valens and J. P. Richardson – the Big Bopper. Also on the bus were former Cricket Tommy Allsup, a long-time friend of Holly's from his home town of Lubbock, Texas, Waylon Jennings and singing group Dion and the Belmonts.

By 2 February 1959 when they played the Surf Ballroom in Clear Lake, Iowa, both Valens and Big Bopper were suffering from colds and Holly could not face the bus journey to their next gig in Moorhead, Minnesota, a journey of several hundred miles. To cut the journey time, he arranged the charter of a plane to Fargo, North Dakota, from where it was a short journey to their destination. The cost was $108 and Holly offered the two remaining seats to anyone in the party who was willing to cough up the required $36 each to cover the cost. Waylon Jennings wanted to fly but gave up his seat to the ailing Big Bopper. Tommy Allsup was also going to fly, but lost his seat on the toss of a coin to Richie Valens. Holly called his young, pregnant wife from a pay-phone in the lobby of the ballroom and Valens phoned his brother. Both complained bitterly about the conditions on the tour.

As they were leaving for the airfield, Holly teased Waylon Jennings about the bus. 'You're not going on that plane tonight?' he joked. Jennings replied that he was taking the bus and Holly retorted, 'Well, I hope your old bus freezes up again!' Jennings shot back, 'Well, I hope your old plane crashes!' They both got their wishes that night.

The plane was a small four-passenger Beechcraft Bonanza, named *American Pie*. It was painted red with a black trim and its pilot, twenty-one-year-old Roger Peterson, was inexperienced and not qualified to fly in difficult conditions.

As the party made its way from Clear Lake to Mason City Airport, the weather was fine, but a weather warning had been issued by the National Weather Service, a warning not received by either Peterson, the pilot, or by Jerry Dwyer who owned the Dwyer Flying Service from whom the plane was being chartered.

The plane took off at around one in the morning into a blinding snowstorm. It came down in a cornfield belonging to Albert Juhl only fifteen miles north-west of Mason City.

All on board were killed instantly.

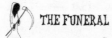 ## THE FUNERAL

The Big Bopper's wake was held in Broussard's Funeral Home, in Beaumont, Texas, where he was buried. Private soldier Elvis Presley and Colonel Tom Parker sent yellow roses to his funeral.

On Saturday 7 February Ritchie Valens' body was taken from the Noble Chapel Funeral Home in the San Fernando Valley, to San Fernando Mission Cemetery. His body was driven in a copper coloured hearse.

Buddy Holly was buried the same day. Services were held in Lubbock, Texas, at the Tabernacle Baptist Church. Over a thousand mourners turned up, but his pregnant widow was unable to attend.

POST MORTEM

- When Jerry Dwyer did not receive news of the safe landing of the plane in Fargo, he became concerned and decided to mount a search. The next morning was foggy which prevented him from flying until about 9 a.m. He finally took off along the same flightpath as the *American Pie* and found the wreckage within five minutes. It had gone unnoticed for eight hours along a fence in that snow-covered field, about a quarter of a mile from the nearest country road.

- Holly had $193 on him when his body was found in the

wreckage. The Mason City coroner took $11.65 of it, for his fees.

- *The Winter Dance Party* tour continued, regardless. The relatively unknown singers Bobby Vee, Paul Anka and Fabian were drafted in to replace Holly, Valens and Big Bopper.
- The crash site became a tourist attraction and some of the visitors to Albert Juhl's field were given souvenir pieces of the wreckage.
- Buddy Holly's wife lost the baby she had been expecting.
- Many years later, Tommy Allsup opened a club which he called The Head's Up Saloon to commemorate the coin toss that saved his life.
- In 1972, Don Maclean had a worldwide hit with the song *American Pie* which was dedicated to the victims of the crash and memorably described that incident as 'the day the music died'. It later became a number one hit for Madonna.
- In 1980, Holly's glasses, four dice and the Big Bopper's watch were discovered in an envelope in the county courthouse at Mason City. They were returned to the families of the deceased.
- In 1990, Gary Busey, who played Buddy Holly in the film *The Buddy Holly Story*, bought one of Holly's guitars at an auction in New York for around $242,000. The Rock and Roll Hall of Fame bought a pair of his glasses for $25,000.
- In 1976, former Beatle Paul McCartney bought the rights to all of Buddy Holly's songs.

— HARRY HOUDINI —

October 1926 was not the best month of Harry Houdini's life. For starters, on the night of 11 October during a performance of his famous Underwater Torture escape, a chain slipped, fracturing his ankle. Houdini characteristically refused the advice of a doctor who was in the audience and stubbornly persevered with his performance, hopping painfully from stunt to stunt on his one good leg and requiring the help of his assistants to finish his tricks. He then ignored doctors' orders that he should rest the leg for two weeks and stubbornly carried on with his tour. During the next two days, he performed in agony, wearing a splint and a leg-brace.

Things got even worse eleven days later, when, opening his mail while lying on a couch in his dressing room in the Princess Theatre in Montreal, Houdini welcomed two students from McGill University who had heard him deliver a lecture the previous week. Preoccupied with his letters, the magician was not paying much attention when one of the boys, J. Gordon Whitehead, a tough six-footer, questioned him about his famous ability to take powerful blows to the stomach. Still reading his post, Houdini began to tell the boy that he could indeed withstand such blows, but he had to brace himself in anticipation of the punch. However, as he stood to prepare himself, the student punched Houdini hard three times in the abdomen without warning. When Whitehead saw the startled look in the magician's eyes, he was shocked, explaining that he thought he had been given permission to throw the punches. Houdini, although in considerable pain, recovered sufficiently to reassure Whitehead and to go onstage for his performance.

Throughout the show, however, it was evident that he was suffering and later that night he admitted to crippling abdominal pain. Arriving for his next engagement in Detroit, he was examined by doctors who diagnosed the pain as a symptom of acute appendicitis. But, even though his temperature had now risen to 102, he still refused to go to hospital, insisting that the show must go on.

Houdini made it through the Detroit performance despite his soaring temperature, his severe abdominal pains and continuing discomfort from his broken ankle. Uncharacteristically, he missed cues and once again his assistants were often called upon to complete tricks for him. At the interval, ice packs were used to try to ease his fever. Just before the third act, however, he turned to his chief assistant, James Collins, and told him to bring down the curtain. He could not go on.

As soon as the curtain dropped, Houdini collapsed onto the stage. He was helped to his dressing room and changed out of his stage clothes, but still refused to go to hospital for treatment, returning, instead, to his hotel.

Early the next morning, 25 October, the illusionist was still in agony and his wife, Bess, insisted on a doctor being called. The hotel physician attended and immediately called a surgeon but Houdini still would not go to hospital until he had spoken to Dr William Stone, his own personal physician whose office was in New York. Stone advised him to listen to what he was being told and Houdini was at last rushed to an operating theatre at Grace Hospital where an operation was performed immediately. His appendix had ruptured, they discovered, causing peritonitis. The doctors informed a shocked Bess that it was unlikely that her husband would survive. They operated again on 29 October, but by this time the sepsis had spread through his system.

Houdini was a tough man and managed to hang on until the early morning of 31 October – Halloween – when, in the darkness of his hospital room, he turned to Bess and his brother, Hardeen, who were at his bedside and whispered: 'I'm getting tired and I can't fight any more.'

He turned his head away and died, aged fifty-two.

 THE FUNERAL

Harry Houdini's body was taken to the funeral home of W. R. Hamilton and Co. in a bronze, silk-lined coffin with a full-length glass top. He had built it himself just four weeks before his death, specifically to use in his act.

A special Pullman car was attached to a train called

The Detroiter, to take him from Michigan Central Station on the night of Monday 1 November. Bess Houdini, in shock since her husband's death, arrived in a wheelchair.

Houdini was buried on 4 November in Machpelah Cemetery, Queens, New York, next to the grave of his mother. Two thousand people attended his funeral and, at his request, he was buried with a collection of his mother's letters beneath the pillow on which his head rested.

POST MORTEM

- It is now thought that Houdini was already suffering from appendicitis when Whitehead punched him. It is likely, however, that he believed his stomach pains were a result of the punches and not appendicitis.
- In the days following his death, there were reports from clairvoyants worldwide who claimed to have predicted that he would die. Amongst them was his former friend Sir Arthur Conan Doyle, with whom he had had a very public disagreement about spiritualism. Conan Doyle's circle had recorded a message about Houdini several months before his death. The message is reported to have said, 'Houdini is doomed, doomed, doomed!'
- Houdini's friend and fellow magician Joseph Dunninger said that on one early morning in October 1926, Houdini called him in New York and asked him to drive over to his house on West 113th Street, as he had to move some things.

When the car was loaded, he asked Dunninger to drive through Central Park. Dunninger said that as they got to the exit on Central Park West, around 72nd Street, Houdini grabbed him by the arm and urged him to go back to his house. When Dunninger asked him if he had forgotten something, Houdini said, 'Don't ask questions, Joe, just turn around and go back.' Arriving at the house, Houdini climbed out of the car and stood looking at it in the rain. He stayed that way for a few minutes and then he got back into the car without saying a word. Dunninger drove off and when the two men again approached the western exit of the park, he glanced over and saw that Houdini's shoulders had started to shake and he was crying. When Dunninger asked him what was wrong Houdini replied, 'I've seen my house for the last time, Joe. I'll never see my house again.' To Dunninger's knowledge, he never did.

• Bess began efforts to honour her husband's requests about attempting contact after death. Every Sunday at the hour of his death, she would shut herself in a room with his photograph and wait for a sign. She made no secret of the fact that she was waiting for a coded message from Houdini and word spread that she had offered $10,000 to any medium who could deliver a true message from the dead illusionist. Every week a new medium would emerge claiming to have broken the code, but no one did until 1928, when the well-known medium Arthur Ford announced that he had a message for Bess. He said it was from Houdini's mother and consisted of just one word – 'forgive'. Bess informed the world that this was the first message she had received that 'had any appearance of truth'. That November Ford received another message, this time from Houdini himself. It was a coded message – 'Rosabelle, answer, tell, pray, answer, look, tell, answer, answer, tell.' It emerged that 'Rosabelle' was the title of a song that had been popular when Bess had first met Houdini. The rest of the message was a series of coded words spelling out the word 'believe'. However, there were accusations that Ford was a fraud, especially as it emerged that the code had been included in a book published in 1927.

• Bess Houdini persevered with what became known as the Houdini Séances. Ten years after his death, the final one, on the roof of the Knickerbocker Hotel in Hollywood, was featured in a worldwide radio broadcast. However, despite their entreaties to the dead magician to lift the table or do something to communicate with them, nothing happened. At the end, a disappointed Bess told the world 'Houdini did not come through. My last hope is gone. I do not believe that Houdini can come back to me – or to anyone. The Houdini shrine has burned for ten years. I now, reverently turn out the light. It is finished. Good night, Harry!' The séance ended, but as it did, a violent thunderstorm erupted, drenching the rooftop gathering and filling the sky with thunder and lightning. Strangely, the storm did not appear anywhere else in Hollywood – only directly above the Knickerbocker Hotel. Houdini Séances continue to this day.

- In 1975, vandals smashed the marble bust on Houdini's grave and it lay in disrepair until it was finally repaired thanks to a donation of $10,000 from a fan, the magician David Copperfield.

— POPE JOHN PAUL II —

John Paul II had been ill for almost a decade. In February 2005, however, his health took a definite turn for the worse. Once an athlete and always a strong speaker, he was now racked with arthritis and Parkinson's disease. Twice in that month he had been rushed to Rome's Gemelli Hospital with breathing problems and had to have a tracheotomy. The operation seemed to drain his strength and, on two occasions, he failed to address crowds in St Peter's Square.

By Thursday 31 March, journalists were being told that the Pope was 'sick, very sick'. On Wednesday he had made a distressing appearance at the window of the Vatican, trying to speak, but emitting only a muffled sound. Doctors had inserted a feeding tube into his stomach to try to boost his energy levels, but he then developed a urinary infection and high fever that soon precipitated heart failure and kidney problems.

His condition was now regarded as 'very serious'. He had received the last rites at 5.17 that Thursday evening and according to Father Konrad Hejmo, a leader of the Polish community in Rome, he was 'ready to die'. He added that the Pontiff was 'fully conscious, lucid and extremely serene'.

The Pope had rejected another visit to hospital, choosing to die in the apartments he had lived in for the twenty-six years of his Pontificate. As Joaquín Navarro-Valls, the director of the Vatican press office, announced the Pope's condition to be 'serious, but stable', up to ten thousand people gathered in St Peter's Square, gazing up at the windows of the Pope's apartments in the Vatican. A fresh update some time later reported that he remained conscious, had celebrated Mass and had asked for the Fourteen Stations of the Cross to be read to him. Navarro-Valls announced that he also asked that the Scripture of the so-called 'Third Hour' be read to him, a passage significant because according to tradition, Christ died at three o'clock in the afternoon. 'This is surely an image I have never seen in these twenty-six years,' the usually unflappable Navarro-Valls said. Breaking down, he had to leave the press conference.

At around five o'clock on Friday evening the Pope's condition worsened; his blood pressure was lower and his breathing had by now become shallow. Cardinal Camillo Ruini, at a special Mass in a Rome cathedral, said that John Paul II was already 'seeing and touching the Lord' and up to seventy thousand people gathered outside the Vatican for an all-night vigil. At times this huge crowd was so silent that the water could be heard trickling down from the fountains in the square. At other times, they sang 'Stay with us!'

Vatican officials denied reports in the media that John Paul was already dead, but speaking to the crowd, Archbishop

Angelo Comastri said: 'This evening, or tonight, Christ is opening the door to the Pope.'

The world prayed for him. In Wadowice, Poland, people left school and work early and went to church to pray for their native son. In the Philippines, special Masses were celebrated. At the Church of the Assumption in Lagos, sub-Saharan Africa's most populous city of over thirteen million, about two hundred Nigerians in Western clothes and bright traditional African robes sat on wooden benches, offering prayers for the Pope at a midday Mass. The White House said President Bush and his wife were praying for him and that the world's concern was 'a testimony to his greatness'. Even China, which bars its Catholics from recognising the authority of the Vatican, expressed concern for the Pope's condition.

On the morning of Saturday 2 April Cardinal Joseph Ratzinger visited the Pope and reported that 'he knows he is dying' and has 'said his last goodbye'. The world watched and waited.

In his last hours, the Pontiff lay in bed amidst a tangle of medical tubes and probes. His long-serving private secretary, Archbishop Dziwisz, did not leave his side and held his hand, while around them, tearful Polish nuns recited the rosary. He was drifting in and out of consciousness but, it was firmly stated, he was not in a coma. His general heart and breathing conditions were by now very serious. At eight o'clock he was once again given the Sacrament for the Sick and Dying – the Last Rites – and listened as his favourite passages from the Scriptures were read.

Shortly after 9.30 on the night of Saturday 2 April John Paul grasped Archbishop Dziwisz's hand and stared at the window of his sparsely furnished bedroom, in the direction of the crowd gathered in St Peter's Square below. As the crowd finished reciting the rosary, he raised his hand to offer a blessing, whispered 'Amen' and died. It was 9.37 p.m.

THE FUNERAL

Rome and large parts of the world came to a stop for the Pope's funeral on a blustery Friday 9 April. Four kings, five queens, one heir to the throne (the Prince of Wales) and seventy presidents and prime ministers attended. St Peter's and its environs were filled with some 350,000 people, mostly young and Slavic, who waved flags and chanted the late Pope's name. 'Santo Subito!' (Sainthood now!) was on their lips. In Krakow, 800,000 people watched the funeral on giant screens.

John Paul's lead-lined coffin was made of cypress wood with a simple cross and the letter M – for 'Mary' – carved into it.

POST MORTEM

- The news of John Paul II's death was immediately announced to the crowds in St Peter's Square and was met with a long applause, an Italian sign of respect. Bells tolled and many people wept openly. 'Our Holy Father, John Paul, has returned to the house of the Father,' Archbishop Leonardo Sandri told the crowds.

- There is a strict ritual after the death of a Pope. A pronouncement is made in Latin that the Pope is dead and is certified by a physician. The Camerlengo, or Chamberlain, the most important Vatican official until a new pope is elected, then calls out the Pontiff's baptismal name – Karol for Pope John Paul II – three times to confirm there is no response. In the past, the Camerlengo struck a silver hammer against the Pope's forehead to confirm his death, but it's unclear if the ritual is still active. The Camerlengo then destroys the symbols of that papacy – the Pescatorio, or Ring of the Fisherman, and the dies used to make lead seals for apostolic letters. The Pope's quarters are sealed and funeral arrangements are begun by the Camerlengo. Vatican flags fly at half-mast and the bronze door of St Peter's Basilica is closed. An official nine-day mourning period, known as the 'novemediales', follows the death of a pope, a tradition dating back to ancient Rome and a ceremony held nine days after death. The Pope's body lies in state in St Peter's Basilica in the Clementine Chapel, which was begun by Michelangelo and completed by Giacomo Della Porta for the Jubilee in 1600. The funeral and burial must be held between the fourth and sixth day after death, according to rules established in 1996 and most popes in recent centuries have chosen to be buried beneath St Peter's Basilica. After the funeral in St Peter's Square, the lead-lined coffin is carried through the 'door of death' on the left side of the main altar in the Basilica. As a single bell is tolled, the coffin is lowered into a marble sarcophagus and covered by a huge stone slab.

- On 19 April, the second day of the Conclave of Cardinals, the hardline German Cardinal Joseph Ratzinger was elected pope on the fourth ballot. It was one of the briefest conclaves of modern times.

⚊ DR DAVID KELLY ⚊

Dr David Kelly's mental state was described by friends and experts as fragile just a few days after the Hutton hearings in which he had been, to his mind at least, humiliated by accusations that he had made allegations to the press that the government hyped intelligence to justify the invasion of Iraq.

Early in the afternoon of 17 July, he decided to go for a walk near his home in the village of Southmoor, some thirty miles south-west of Oxford. The last person to see him alive was Ruth Absolom, an elderly neighbour, as she walked her dog, Buster.

She admitted her surprise later at his suicide because he seemed 'absolutely normal', telling the inquest jury, 'We just stopped and said hello, had a chat. He said "Hello Ruth." I said "Hello David, how are things?" He said, "Not too bad." We stood there for a few moments and then Buster, my dog, was pulling on the lead, he wanted to get going. I said "I will have to go, David." He said "See you again, then, Ruth." And that was it, we parted.' He seemed to her: 'Just his normal self, no different to any other time when I met him.'

When Dr Kelly left Mrs Absolom, he walked on to a remote

beauty spot in the Harrowdown Hills and it was there that he took his life.

His body was found slumped against the foot of a tree in a wooded copse with his left wrist slashed. The Scout knife he had owned since childhood was by his side along with a bottle of his wife's painkillers and a bottle of water. He had removed his cap and watch. There were no signs of a struggle.

 THE FUNERAL

David Kelly's funeral took place on Wednesday 6 August 2003, at St Mary's Church, Longworth, Oxfordshire. Thames Valley Police cordoned off parts of Longworth and Southmoor and the casket was decorated with white roses and lilies together with the insignia of the Order of St Michael and St George, awarded in recognition of his services to Britain and the United Nations.

There were 160 mourners, amongst whom were John Prescott, the Deputy Prime Minister, and Lord Hutton who led the subsequent inquiry into the scientist's death. Bells were rung at other churches across the country.

The ceremony was predominantly Anglican but contained a reading from the texts of the Baha'i faith, adopted by Dr Kelly four years before his death. There was also a poem by Wilfred Hawe-Nurse, a resident of Longworth, reflecting Dr Kelly's love of his adopted home as well as a Welsh hymn in recognition of the land of his birth. Following the service, his body was buried in the churchyard.

 **POST MORTEM**

- Two volunteer search and rescue experts discovered the body of Dr Kelly in the early hours of 18 July. They had been drafted into the search for the scientist by the police who were eager to make use of their dog, Brock, and his training as a hearing dog for the deaf.

- Brock had picked up 'something obviously not quite the same as a normal search or a normal training exercise' because instead of taking his handler to the scene, he lay down on the ground and looked up. She went deeper into the wood to investigate and saw the body of Dr Kelly, dressed in a shirt and jeans, slumped against the bottom of a tree. She explained that his legs were straight in front of him, his right arm was to the side of him, his left arm had a lot of blood on it and was bent back in a funny position.

- Two paramedics told the inquiry they had tried to pick up a pulse from Dr Kelly's body by attaching electrocardiogram pads to his chest, but failed as he had been dead for some time. Vanessa Hunt, one of the paramedics, said: 'On his left arm, which was outstretched to the left of him, there was some dried blood.'

- Detective Sergeant Geoffrey Webb of Thames Valley Police discovered various pieces of documentation in Dr Kelly's study after his death relating to the Iraq issue, including an unopened letter of reprimand from the MoD.

- Dr Kelly was a convert to the Baha'i faith and Barney Leith, the secretary of the National Spiritual Assembly of the Baha'is, said its website was 'clarifying the issue' of suicide. He said although Baha'i teaching condemned suicide, it did not take a condemnatory attitude to people who take their own lives.

- The scientist's GP, Dr Malcolm Warner, told the inquiry he had not seen Dr Kelly for four years and that his patient had no history of depression.

- Professor Keith Hawton, a consultant psychiatrist and the director of the Centre for Suicide Research at Oxford University, carried out a detailed investigation into Dr Kelly's death. He said Dr Kelly's 'normal' behaviour on the day he died was 'consistent with the notion he had made his decision before that to end his life or try to end his life'. Professor Hawton said that among people who had committed suicide, it was not unusual for those who knew them to say that their mental state seemed improved: 'It is having, in a sense, decided how to deal with the problem that leads to a sort of sense of peace and calm.' Professor Hawton described the scientist from his conversations with his widow, Janice, as 'shocked, broken and humiliated'. He added: 'One gains the impression of escalating distress during that morning. I think, as far as we can deduce, the major factor was the severe loss of self-esteem resulting from his feeling people had lost trust in him and from his dismay at being exposed to the media … being such a private man this was anathema to him to be exposed publicly, and in a sense he would have seen it as being publicly disgraced.'

— STAN LAUREL —

The great comedy duo Laurel and Hardy appeared together in public for the last time, on British television, in 1955, talking about the British performers they had known, for a programme about the charitable Variety organisation the Grand Order of Water Rats. It had been a tough few years for them. In 1950, they had travelled to France to make a film, a Franco-Italian production called *Atoll K*. It had been a disaster. Language problems and the failing health of both stars, especially Laurel, ensured its failure and it would be the last film the two would make.

Their previous career, however, had been stellar. Born Arthur Stanley Jefferson in Ulverton in Lancashire, Laurel had gone to America with Fred Karno's troupe, eventually deciding to be a writer and director in the new medium of film. A chance pairing with versatile actor Oliver Norvell Hardy persuaded him that his future lay in front of the camera.

After 150 films, however, spanning both the silent and talkie eras, it was time to wind down and Hardy, suffering from a heart condition, was told to take it easy and lose weight. He lost over 100 pounds in 1956, but suffered several strokes, possibly as a result of such dramatic weight loss. On 7 August 1957, 'Babe' as he was known, had a massive stroke and died, weighing a mere 138 pounds.

Stan Laurel was, naturally, devastated. He did not attend his friend's funeral as his own health was in such a precarious state, saying simply: 'Babe would understand.'

He lived for another eight years, but refused to tread the boards again. In 1961, he received a special Academy Award and he did write gags for several directors. He answered every fan letter sent to him personally and fans were astonished to find that if they called his number, they would find themselves talking to Stan Laurel himself.

The new generation of comedians beat a path to the door of his small apartment in the Oceana Hotel in Santa Monica, seeking advice during his twilight years – Dick Cavett, Dick Van Dyke and Jerry Lewis amongst them. In 1965, however, he finally succumbed to his poor health. He suffered a heart attack in mid February and was rushed to hospital.

A few days later, he told a nurse who was attending to him that he would love to go skiing. Puzzled, the nurse replied that she did not know that he was a skier. 'I'm not,' said the great comedian, 'I'd rather be doing that than have all these needles stuck into me!'

It would be his last joke. When she looked at him a few minutes later, he was dead, aged seventy-five.

 # THE FUNERAL

Stan Laurel was buried at Forest Lawn Hollywood Hills Cemetery in Los Angeles. Dick Van Dyke delivered the eulogy. Comedy greats such as Buster Keaton, Patsy Kelly, Alan Mowbray, Tim Conway, Pat Butram, Babe London and Hal Roach Jr were present. Buster Keaton was heard to say: 'Chaplin wasn't the funniest, I wasn't the funniest, this man was the funniest.' Laurel had told his friends: 'If any of you have a long face at my funeral, I'll never talk to you again.'

 # POST MORTEM

In 1989 a statue of Stan Laurel was erected in Dockwray Square, North Shields, Northumberland, England where he lived at No. 8 from 1897 until 1902.

T. E. LAWRENCE, 'LAWRENCE OF ARABIA'

After the global fame his desert exploits had brought him, T. E. Lawrence's descent into the ranks had bemused people. To George Bernard Shaw, it was as if Nelson, after the Battle of the Nile, had insisted on being put at the tiller of a canal barge; according to him, it was 'a maddening masquerade'. But Lawrence simply loved being in the Royal Air Force. He told one journalist: 'I'm in the RAF because I like it and when people offer me larger boots and talk of my wasting my "talents" in the ranks, I comfort myself with the sure knowledge that there's nothing else my talented self wants to do.'

Therefore, it was with no little distress that he arrived at the end of his RAF career – 'the only really contented years of my life' as he described them. He had been moved about the country in the last few years and now, in 1935, back at Clouds Hill, the cottage he had purchased for himself about a mile from Bovington camp in Dorset, he was forced to ease himself into frugal retirement. At Clouds Hill, he received visitors from the artistic and literary world. Here, too, he engaged another private, John Bruce, to birch him severely every day, a ritual his brother ascribed to the methods used by saints to purge them-selves of the urge for sex.

Some tried to get him back into public life. In one of the last letters he received, Lady Astor, a close friend, wrote to him: 'If you come to Cliveden the last Saturday in May you will never regret it.' Listing the people who would be there – Stanley Baldwin, who had been prime minister and was about to be again, among them – she suggested that the government would be keen for him to take part in the reorganisation of the armed forces. Characteristically, Lawrence replied: 'No. Wild mares would not at present take me away from Clouds Hill. It is an earthly paradise and I am staying here until I feel qualified for it. Also there is something broken in the works, as I told you: my will, I think. In this mood I would not take on any job at all. So do not commit yourself to advocating me, lest I prove a non-starter.'

Henry Williamson, author of *Tarka the Otter* and a close friend of Lawrence, was a supporter of Oswald Mosley's British Fascist Movement and had displayed some sympathy for Adolf Hitler. He had been deeply moved by his experiences on the Western Front in World War I and feared that another war between Britain and Germany would bring the end of civilisation and the unstoppable rise of Bolshevism. He wrote to Lawrence at the beginning of May asking him whether he would be interested in meeting Hitler, believing that the Führer could be influenced by a man like Lawrence. Lawrence answered by telegram, inviting Williamson to lunch at Clouds Hill. It was the last correspondence he wrote.

Pat Knowles lived across the road from Clouds Hill and was a friend and aide to Lawrence. He described the morning of Tuesday 13 May as Lawrence set out to post his telegram to Williamson. 'He came across to me shortly before he went and asked if there was anything I wanted and shortly afterwards I heard him move off. Well, it was one of those bright, clear days in May when the wind was southerly and it was very pleasant, and I could hear the drill sergeants on the squares. And later I heard the motorcycle coming back. I heard the engine suddenly race and then stop.'

On the road from Bovington Camp, Lawrence had been forced to swerve to avoid two errand boys. He clipped the wheel of one of their bikes and lost control of his Brough (the seventh Brough he had owned in the past twelve years, all called by the biblical name 'Boanerges' – 'the sons of thunder'). He flew over the handlebars of the motorbike and hit the ground hard, knocking himself unconscious.

Lawrence lay in a coma for six days at Bovington Camp Hospital before dying shortly after eight on the morning of Sunday 19 May. He was forty-six years old.

 ## THE FUNERAL

Lawrence was buried at Moreton Church, near Clouds Hill, on 21 May 1935. He had expressly requested that there be no wreaths or flowers.

His pall-bearers were British diplomat Sir Ronald Storrs,

the artist Eric Kennington, Colonel Stewart F. Newcombe, Aircraftman Bradbury – a friend of Lawrence, Arthur Russell of the Tank Corps and Pat Knowles.

Amongst the mourners were Winston Churchill, Lady Astor and the artist Augustus John. The only biographical detail in the inscription on the headstone states that he had been a Fellow of All Souls College, Oxford.

☠ POST MORTEM

- An oak tree commemorates the spot on the road to Bovington where Lawrence crashed. It reads: 'Near this spot Lawrence of Arabia crashed on his motorcycle and was fatally injured 13 May 1935. This tree was planted on 13 May 1983 by Mr Tom Beaumont who served with Lawrence in Arabia as his No. 1 Vickers Machine Gunner.'
- Clouds Hill Cottage is now a museum.

‒ BRANDON LEE ‒

In March 1993, filming of *The Crow*, starring twenty-eight-year-old Brandon Lee, was nearing completion at Carolco Studios in Wilmington, North Carolina. It had been a troublesome shoot, accidents plaguing the set before and after shooting. On 1 February, the first day of shooting, a carpenter had received serious burns when a scissor lift he was driving hit some high-voltage power lines. On 13 March, severe storms had destroyed a number of the elaborate sets. Other mishaps included a disgruntled carpenter driving his car into the studio's plaster shop, one worker accidentally stabbing his hand with a screwdriver and a stunt man breaking several ribs after plunging through a roof.

Eight days before the completion of the film, Brandon Lee, son of the late martial arts movie phenomenon Bruce Lee, was due to film a scene that involved a close-up scene of a gun being fired. Dummy cartridges were to be used in the scene. These are perfect for close-up shots because they contain the actual projectile but no gunpowder. Therefore, it looks as if there are real bullets in the chamber.

On the day in question, however, the studio's props department had run out of dummy cartridges. To save time and money, therefore – the production would have to be shut down for the night if they had to wait for the cartridges to be delivered – it was decided to remove the gunpowder from live rounds and replace the bullet tips.

The close-up scenes were completed and the dummy bullets were replaced with blanks loaded with highly explosive powder that would create the smoke and flash that a real gun would give. This was what was needed for the next scene which called for a wide shot of Lee's character being shot. He was required to enter a room where actor Michael Massee was to fire the gun. Fatally, no one from the inexperienced crew thought to check the gun's barrel.

'Action!' was called and Lee, dressed in a black leather jacket and boots, and a t-shirt bearing the phrase 'Hangman's Joke', entered the room carrying a bag of groceries. Massee fired the gun at him from a distance of about fifteen feet and Lee set off the 'squib', a device to simulate bullets hitting the bag he was carrying. Tragically, however, when the dummies had been put in the revolver, a piece of one of the bullets that had been tampered with by the props department had broken off and become lodged in the barrel or cylinder. It hit Lee.

He collapsed, blood pouring from his right side. He groaned and signalled with his arm that he had been hit, but no one noticed. It was only when the director shouted 'Cut!' and the actor failed to rise that they realised there was a problem.

An ambulance rushed him to the nearby New Hanover Regional Medical Center. He was still alive despite the large wound in his right abdomen and serious damage to his stomach and vital organs. The bullet had finally come to rest next to his spine and it was decided to perform emergency surgery to stop the severe internal haemorrhaging.

But their efforts were futile and Brandon Lee died in the hospital at three minutes past one on the afternoon of 31 March 1993, a little more than twelve hours after the shooting.

 ## THE FUNERAL

His body was flown back to Washington State where he was buried on 3 April next to his father in Lake View Cemetery. The next day a memorial service was held at the house of his actress friend Polly Bergen, in the Hollywood Hills. Amongst those attending were David Carradine, Kiefer Sutherland, David Hasselhoff, Lou Diamond Phillips and Steven Seagal.

 ## POST MORTEM

- The subsequent investigation failed to conclusively determine how the bullet tip had become dislodged. The blank cartridge had enough force when fired to propel the bullet tip into the young actor's body.
- Investigators concluded that it was an accidental death caused by negligence on the part of the film crew.
- Linda Lee Cauldwell, Brandon Lee's mother, filed a civil suit against the studio, but it was settled out of court.

- Both Lee's mother and his fiancée, Eliza Hutton, were in favour of the completion of the film. This required some rewrites, shooting remaining scenes with a double and putting Lee's face into a few key scenes digitally. Paramount Pictures were concerned about marketing the film and after several other studios declined, Miramax, renowned for selling difficult, small, independent films, took it on. They did not use Lee's death in any way and the only mention is in the closing credits where there is a dedication 'For Brandon and Eliza'. *The Crow* was eventually released on 11 May 1994. Unsurprisingly, it did well at the box office with final takings of over $50 million.
- Some say that the scene where Brandon Lee was killed is still in the final film. However, this is unlikely to be true and it is believed the section of film in question was destroyed.

 ### THE CONSPIRACY THEORY

- Brandon Lee believed his family was jinxed by a curse made against his grandfather when he angered some Chinese businessmen.
- Some people claim that he was murdered by the same Chinese Mafia that are said to have caused the 1973 death of his father as punishment for his exposure of ancient martial arts secrets on film.
- Others say that Brandon Lee was murdered by gangsters with ties to the Hong Kong movie industry, who had been angered by his refusal to work in their films.

‒ BRUCE LEE ‒

In May 1973, during the final dubbing of Bruce Lee's film *Enter the Dragon*, the martial arts actor suffered a sudden attack of seizures and a cerebral oedema. Fortunately, the attack was not fatal but the neurosurgeon who saved his life, Dr Peter Wu, said that he removed a considerable amount of hashish from Lee's stomach. He had been chewing hashish to calm himself in the face of escalating international celebrity.

On 20 July 1973, Lee was busying himself with ideas for his next film, *Game of Death*, and around two in the afternoon, he held a meeting at home with film producer Raymond Chow. The two men worked until four and then drove to the apartment of Betty Taipei, a Taiwanese actress who was to be one of the stars of the film. The three worked on the script before Chow had to leave for a meeting, agreeing to meet them for dinner later with the former James Bond star George Lazenby, with whom Lee was planning to make a film.

Lee had been complaining of a headache and Taipei gave him a pill containing equagesic, a kind of super-aspirin. He had consumed nothing other than a couple of soft drinks.

At around 7.30, he lay down to have a nap and was still

asleep when Chow called to ask why the pair had not turned up for dinner as arranged. Taipei told Chow that she had tried to wake Lee, but had been unable to do so. Chow hurried over to the apartment and, also failing to wake the actor, immediately summoned medical help. After trying to revive Lee for ten minutes, an ambulance was called to take him to Queen Elizabeth Hospital.

He was dead on arrival, aged just thirty-two.

THE FUNERAL

In Hong Kong, thousands lined the streets to honour his symbolic burial parade and scores of spectators were injured in the crush. Steel barriers were erected along the coffin's route to restrain the crowd.

Pall-bearers at Lee's funeral in Seattle in July 1973 included Steve McQueen, James Coburn, Chuck Norris and George Lazenby. He was laid to rest in Lakeview Cemetery, wearing the traditional Chinese outfit he wore in *Enter the Dragon*.

POST MORTEM

- Foul play was immediately suspected. Raymond Chow appeared on television to try to settle the public furore that quickly developed. He explained what happened, omitting only the fact that Lee had not died at home. The press soon uncovered the truth, however, and demanded to know what Chow was trying to cover up, sensing that the actor had been having an affair with Taipei.

- He died of a brain aneurysm in the vicinity of the cerebral oedema that had first surfaced in May 1973. Whether it was present from birth or caused later by a blow to the head is unknown. In any case, he was living on borrowed time with a damaged blood vessel in his head capable of exploding at any moment.

- Medical authorities came up with five reasons for his death. They all agreed that it was caused by a cerebral oedema – a swelling of the brain caused by a congestion of fluid – but what caused the oedema was not so certain. The ensuing autopsy found traces of cannabis in Lee's stomach, but the significance of this discovery is debatable. Some believe the cannabis caused a chemical reaction that led to the oedema, but the coroner's inquiry refutes this theory. In fact, one doctor was quoted as saying that the cannabis in Lee's stomach was 'no more significant than if Bruce had drunk a cup of tea that day'.

- Dr R. R. Lycette of Queen Elizabeth Hospital concluded that Lee's death resulted from a hypersensitivity to one or more of the compounds found in the headache tablet he had consumed that afternoon. Although his skull showed no injury, his brain had swollen considerably, from 1,400 to 1,575 grams. None of the blood vessels were blocked or broken, and the possibility of a haemorrhage was ruled out. All of his internal organs were meticulously examined, and the only 'foreign' substance to be found was the equagesic.

He concluded that Lee was very vulnerable to the effects of drugs due to his extremely low body fat. Dr Donald Langford, Lee's physician in Hong Kong, said that his body had less than one per cent body fat, declaring that 'it was obscene how little body fat he had'. The actor weighed only around 128 pounds at the time of his death.

- R. D. Teare, a professor of forensic medicine at the University of London who had overseen more than ninety thousand autopsies, was called in and declared that it was impossible for cannabis to be a factor in Lee's death. In Teare's opinion, the oedema was caused by hypersensitivity to either meprobamate or aspirin, or a combination of both. His view was accepted by the authorities, and a verdict of 'misadventure' was given.

 ## THE CONSPIRACY THEORY

Speculation was rife that Bruce Lee had been killed by:

- Hong Kong Triads because he refused to pay them the protection money that Chinese film stars were expected to pay.
- An angry martial artist's *dim mak* (death touch) strike in a challenge match because he had given up the secrets of the martial arts community by teaching foreigners.
- *Oni* – Japanese demons or evil spirits.
- The curse of a haunted house that he had just bought in Hong Kong.

VLADIMIR ILYCH — ULYANOV-LENIN —

The health of Vladimir Ilich Ulyanov-Lenin, Chairman of the Council of People's Commissars – leader of the Soviet Union – had never been great, but by mid 1921 it was in drastic decline. He was suffering from severe headaches and insomnia and had been the victim of a series of small heart attacks. Distressingly for a workaholic like him, it was becoming increasingly diffi-cult to put in a full day's work. When he informed the Politburo about his problems, he was instructed to take time off.

He did so, but managed to set up a regime which allowed him to carry on working for a time, if not at full stretch, in the place known as the 'Big House' in Gorki. As time went on, however, for the first time in his life, Lenin began to lose the will to work and his doctors seemed unable to diagnose what was wrong with him. He endured frequent episodes of obses-siveness and wondered whether he was, in fact, going mad. Above all, however, Lenin feared a lingering death. To allay his fears, he solicited a promise from his comrade, Stalin, to give him poison should he request it.

He returned to the Kremlin where the diagnoses were

whittled down eventually to just a few – syphilis; neurasthenia or nervous exhaustion; residual damage from an operation he had undergone to remove a bullet from his neck, and cerebral arteriosclerosis, the illness which had killed his father.

On 5 March 1923, his condition worsened and by 7 March he was beginning to lose the use of the extremities on the right side of his body. Soon, he was unable to speak and had to be carried everywhere. On 10 March, a huge spasm took away all the movement from his right side and he could only move his left hand with difficulty. Worse, he had to endure unbearable headaches.

On 15 May 1923, he was moved once again from the Kremlin to the 'Big House' and, apart from several excursions – one of them to the Kremlin for the last time – that was where he remained.

By 21 January 1924, there was cause for hope, however. Lenin had not had a collapse for a month and had even been getting about with the help of a stick. However, waking at 10.30 a.m. that morning, he complained of feeling unwell while drinking some black coffee. He went back to bed and slept until three o'clock in the afternoon. Feeling better when he woke, he drank a little more coffee and sipped some clear soup. His physician, Dr Osipov, found nothing to worry about when he went to Lenin's room to carry out his daily examination. The leader's pulse was a little fast, but that was all.

Then, around 5.40 p.m., Lenin, propped up in bed, felt the onset of an attack. The three doctors on duty – Osipov, Förster and Yelistratov – and their assistant, Vladimir Rukavishnikov, held a hasty consultation, but there was little they could do but watch as Lenin slipped into a coma. It was not the first time this had happened, but this time he stayed in it much longer than before. When his heartbeat was found to be slowing down, Maria Ilinichna, his younger sister, sent out for camphor to help restore it.

Fellow Politburo member Nikolai Bukharin was staying at the 'Big House' and, hearing that something was happening, ran across to investigate. By this time, Lenin's temperature had risen sharply and, covered in sweat, he tossed and turned in his narrow bed, roaring in pain. Bukharin wrote: 'When I ran into Ilich's room, full of doctors and stacked with medicines, Ilich let out a last sigh. His face fell back and went terribly white. He let out a wheeze, his hands dropped. Ilich, Ilich was no more.'

The doctors lifted his eyelids, looking for signs of life, but Vladimir Ilich Ulyanov-Lenin's struggle was finally over. It was 6.50 p.m.

 ## THE FUNERAL

On 23 January 1924, Lenin's coffin was taken by train to Moscow. His corpse was laid out in the House of Trade Unions and mourners flooded into the capital from all over the USSR.

The funeral, on 27 January, took place on the coldest day of the year – so cold that the trumpeters had to smear vodka on their mouthpieces to prevent them from freezing to their lips.

Amongst the pall-bearers were Zinoviev, Stalin, Bukharin and Molotov. The entire country came to a standstill. Trains stopped in their tracks and factory whistles and hooters sounded in all the towns and villages of the USSR. At four o'clock on a dark afternoon, Lenin was lowered into the earth in a vault that had been prepared in front of the Kremlin in Red Square.

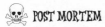 POST MORTEM

- On the orders of the Politburo, Lenin's body was dug up and kept on ice in the Central Moscow mortuary until scientists had worked out how to embalm it so that it could be put on permanent display in a mausoleum in Red Square. The Bolshevik leadership claimed it was only responding to requests by factory workers but, in reality, it was Stalin's idea. He thought that it would serve as a unifying presence for citizens of the Soviet Union as well as for communists around the world.

- Petrograd, formerly St Petersburg, was renamed Leningrad in his honour.

- An Institute of the Brain was established in his honour and thirty thousand slices of his brain tissue were collected so that research might be carried out on the secrets of his genius.

- The Mausoleum Group, responsible for looking after Lenin's body, also mummified and helps to maintain the bodies of Mao Zedong and Ho Chi Minh. Some say that in the basement of his tomb they keep Lenin lookalikes in case his body crumbles. This is denied.

— LIBERACE —

He was born Wladziu Valentino Liberace but, when he was not being called 'Mr Showmanship', 'the Candelabra Kid', 'Mr Box Office', 'the Guru of Glitter' or – close friends only – 'Lee', he was known by just the one name – Liberace.

He had been a precocious child prodigy, playing piano by ear at the age of four, and at the age of twenty made his solo debut with the Chicago Symphony Orchestra. Soon, his signature candelabra glittering on his grand piano, he was tickling the ivories in his semi-classical fashion in clubs and hotels across America. By 1950, his name changed to simply Liberace, he had added an element of comedy and some singing to his act, as well as flamboyant clothes and began to be a regular on the new medium of television. *The Dinah Shore Show* was America's biggest at the time and Liberace's appearances between 1952 and 1956 made him a huge star. In 1955, he became the highest paid performer in Las Vegas, earning $50,000 a week. By the 1960s, he was America's highest-paid entertainer, earning in the region of $5 million a year.

In a time when disclosure of homosexuality was guaranteed to bring down the final curtain on a performer's career,

Liberace's sexual tendencies were a subject of great speculation. Nonetheless, he resolutely denied being gay, to the extent of taking British tabloid newspaper the *Daily Mirror* to court when it hinted he might just conceivably not be completely heterosexual. Its columnist Cassandra described the entertainer as a 'deadly, winking, sniggering, snuggling, chromium-plated, scent-impregnated, luminous, quivering, giggling, fruit-flavoured, mincing, ice-covered heap of mother love ... a sugary mountain of jingling claptrap wrapped in such a preposterous clown'. Liberace denied everything and won.

In 1982, his closet door swung wide open when his former lover of five years, Scott Thorson, whose face Liberace's plastic surgeon had remodelled to make him look like the pianist, sued him for palimony of $113,000,000. Liberace denied Thorson's accusations before settling out of court for $95,000. No slouch in sleaze, Thorson would later claim to have had a relationship with Michael Jackson and was a key prosecution witness in a notorious American quadruple murder case known as the Wonderland murders.

By 1980, Liberace had found another love – eighteen-year-old Cary James. However, in 1985, the couple tested HIV-positive. Liberace was ill and had lost fifty pounds in weight. His condition was not helped by his shock at the death of his old friend Rock Hudson, the actor and fellow closet homosexual, with whom he is reputed to have had a relationship. Still, as he rehearsed for his last-ever concert, at Radio City Music Hall, Liberace refused to admit that he was gay. To close friends, he said, 'I don't want to be remembered as an old queen who died of AIDS.' To the outside world, his management attributed the weight loss to the 'watermelon diet' that was all the rage in Hollywood at the time.

When, in January 1987, Liberace's sister Angelina realised that her brother was very ill indeed, she insisted on him being taken to the Eisenhower Medical Center in Rancho Mirage, Riverside County, California. He was immediately quarantined, confirming to the expectant members of the press that the pianist was, indeed, suffering from AIDS. Three days later, he returned to his lavishly appointed house at 226 Alejo Road in Palm Springs where the media swarmed and almost a hundred of his most ardent fans waited for news. He had come home to die.

Reportedly, he saw out his last hours watching reruns of his favourite television show, *The Golden Girls*, in the company of his sister, Angelina, his sister-in-law, Dora, widow of his beloved brother George, a man called Jamie Wyatt, described as his 'friend and long-time companion' and his twenty-seven dogs.

He died at 2.05 p.m. on 4 February 1987. He was sixty-seven years old.

 THE FUNERAL

Liberace was buried on 7 February in Forest Lawn Cemetery in Hollywood Hills in Los Angeles. Robert Goulet delivered a eulogy and the pianist was buried wearing his wig, a white tuxedo and full stage make-up. Photos of his last boyfriend and Wrinkles, his favourite of all his dogs, were placed in the casket with him.

His extravagant tombstone is made of white marble and a classical statue stands on top of it. It is decorated with his signature complete with sketched grand piano and his trademark candelabra. His brother George and his mother lie beside him.

POST MORTEM

- Liberace's doctors listed his cause of death as 'cardiac arrest due to cardiac failure, due to sub-acute encephalopathy with a contributing condition of aplastic anaemia'. His body was swiftly removed to the Forest Lawn Cemetery in Los Angeles County for burial but, knowing that the entertainer was suffering from AIDS, the coroner in Riverside County insisted on the body being brought back for an autopsy. Coroner Raymond Carillo stated subsequently at a news conference that Liberace had actually died of 'cytomegalovirus pneumonia due to human immunodeficiency virus disease ... an opportunistic disease caused by acquired immune deficiency syndrome'. He continued: 'Cytomegalovirus is a common virus that affects more than half the adult population without ill effects. However, it can be fatal to people whose immune system is weakened by the

AIDS virus.' He accused Liberace's doctors of covering up the real cause of death.

- Other ailments contributing to Liberace's death included lung and heart disease and a hardening of a valve in the heart.

— ABRAHAM LINCOLN —

Friday 14 April 1865 was a beautiful spring day. As usual, Abraham Lincoln, the sixteenth President of the United States, rose at seven. He was feeling good as he sat down at his mahogany desk to deal with some work before breakfast. A few days previously, his general, Ulysses Grant, had accepted the surrender of Robert E. Lee, Commander-in-Chief of the Confederate armies, and Lincoln was now awaiting news that another southern general, Joseph E. Johnston, had also capitulated in North Carolina.

Lincoln gave instructions for Assistant Secretary of State Frederick Seward to call a Cabinet meeting for eleven o'clock that morning and wrote a message inviting General Grant to attend. At eight, Lincoln had breakfast — always one egg and one cup of coffee — with his wife, Mary, and his sons, Robert and Tad, before returning to work in his office.

The papers that morning announced that the President, along with General Grant and his wife, would be attending the comedy *Our American Cousin* at Ford's Theater that evening and Lincoln sent a messenger to the theatre to reserve the state box for him and his party.

At the end of the Cabinet meeting, around two o'clock, however, Grant informed Lincoln that he and his wife had decided to visit their children and were no longer able to go to the theatre. Secretary of War Stanton, overhearing plans for the theatre visit, pleaded with the President not to endanger himself by going out at night – these were unstable times. Lincoln himself became reluctant to attend, as he told his wife over lunch, but he soon changed his mind and invited Major Henry Rathbone and his fiancée, Clara Harris, to join them.

Finishing work around four in the afternoon, he and Mary enjoyed a carriage ride but, later, after dinner, Mary complained of a headache and again considered not going to the theatre. Lincoln demurred, complaining that he was a little tired, but then said he needed cheering up and would go without her. Mary again changed her mind and decided she would accompany him after all.

Still anxious for news from North Carolina, Lincoln, accompanied by his bodyguard William Crook, made his way to the War Department, but nothing had been heard. On their return journey, Crook joined the voices fearful for the President's safety, begging him to cancel the theatre visit. When Lincoln rejected his pleas, Crook asked if he could go along as extra security. Again, Lincoln refused his request, believing that with a guard posted outside the state box in the theatre he would be safe.

It was shortly after eight when the Lincolns left for Ford's

Theater. Mary was wearing a black and white striped silk dress and a matching bonnet and the President wore white kid gloves and a black overcoat made of wool, tailored for him by Brooks Brothers of New York. They took their seats after the play had started but the performance stopped as the orchestra burst into a rendition of *Hail to the Chief*. The door to the box was then closed but, crucially, not locked. Moreover, unluckily for the President, John Parker, the police guard that night, was a man who was fond of a drink and, true to form, at the interval, Parker abandoned his post in the hallway that led to the President's box and walked across the road to the Taltavul's Star Saloon. When the play's third act began he had still not returned to his post.

Mary sat very close to her husband, holding his hand. She whispered to him, 'What will Miss Harris think of my hanging on to you so?' The President replied, 'She won't think anything about it.' It was about 10.15 and, on stage, actor Harry Hawk was saying, 'Don't know the manners of good society, eh? Well, I guess I know enough to turn you inside out, old gal – you sockdologizing old mantrap!'

At this point, the door to the box opened and Lincoln's assassin, the ex-actor John Wilkes Booth, leapt in, pointed a derringer at the back of the President's head and pulled the trigger. As Mary screamed and reached out to her husband as he slumped forward in his seat, the man pulled out a dagger, yelling: 'Sic semper tyrannis!' ('Thus always to tyrants'). He slashed Rathbone's arm to the bone and then leapt from the box, catching his spur in a flag and breaking his left shin as he crashed to the stage. Limping badly, he managed to escape through the rear stage door.

The unconscious Lincoln had been shot behind the left ear, the bullet tearing through that side of his brain. He was carried across the street to the house of a German tailor, William A. Petersen, and into the room of a War Department clerk where, breathing heavily, he had to be laid on the bed diagonally as he was too tall for it.

Six surgeons were present, one of whom, Dr Hall, announced that the President was already, to all intents and purposes, dead, but that he might live another three hours or so. He had been stripped of his clothes and his face was calm, although, after a while, his right eye began to swell and his face became discoloured.

The Speaker of the Senate and other members of the Cabinet arrived and a guard was posted at the door, as there was a large, excitable crowd gathering outside. This room, like every other room in the house, was by now full to overflowing.

Every hour Mrs Lincoln would return to her husband's bedside. At around seven in the morning, she visited his bedside for the last time. Lincoln's son Robert stood at the head of the bed, sobbing.

At 7.22 on the morning of 15 April 1865, President Abraham Lincoln expired, lying diagonally on a strange bed, much too small for his giant frame.

 THE FUNERAL

Lincoln's funeral train left Washington on 21 April 1865 to retrace the 1,654-mile route he had travelled as President-elect in 1861. The *Lincoln Special*, whose engine had Lincoln's photograph over the cowcatcher, carried approximately three hundred mourners. His son Willie's coffin was also on board. Willie, who had died in the White House in 1862 at the age of eleven, had been disinterred and was to be buried with his father in Springfield. A guard of honour accompanied the remains. Robert Lincoln rode on the train to Baltimore but then returned to Washington.

In Baltimore, approximately ten thousand people viewed the coffin in three hours. Forty thousand people lined the streets of Harrisburg as it passed. In Philadelphia it was estimated that three hundred thousand people filed past the coffin and in New York the number was five hundred thousand. Hundreds of thousands of people viewed it as it was borne across the Union before finally being laid to rest in Springfield.

POST MORTEM

- After exiting Ford's Theater, John Wilkes Booth mounted a horse that was being held by an innocent theatre employee and escaped to the south. On 26 April he was shot dead by Boston Corbett of the Sixteenth New York Cavalry unit near Bowling Green, Virginia.

- Eight conspirators were tried for Lincoln's assassination. All were found guilty and four hanged, including Mary Surratt, the first woman executed by the US government.

- A few days before his death, Lincoln told his wife of a dream he had in which he saw a funeral in the White House. 'Who is dead?' he asked a soldier. 'The President, killed by an assassin!' was the soldier's reply.

- Edwin Booth, John Wilkes Booth's brother, died on 7 June 1893. Two days later, at the very moment Edwin's casket was being carried from the Little Church Around the Corner in New York City, all three floors of Ford's Theater collapsed, killing twenty-two people and injuring sixty-eight others.

- The young couple (Henry Rathbone and Clara Harris) who attended *Our American Cousin* with the Lincolns, were married two years after the assassination and had three children. Rathbone suffered from severe mood swings and was probably taking an opiate that could be purchased over the counter in nineteenth-century America. In 1882 he was appointed to the post of US Consul General to Germany but on 23 December 1883, he went berserk, trying to kill his children, then shooting and stabbing his wife to death, before finally stabbing himself. He spent the rest of his life in an asylum for the criminally insane.

- In May 1875, an insanity trial for Mary Todd Lincoln, the President's wife, was held in Chicago. The jury found Mrs Lincoln 'insane and a fit person to be in a state hospital for the insane'. Mary spent the next several months in an asylum in Batavia, Illinois.

- William A. Petersen, the German tailor in whose house the President died, committed suicide. His body, filled with laudanum (a mixture of alcohol and opium derivatives), was found in the grounds of the Smithsonian Institute on 18 June 1871.

- Robert Lincoln, the President's son, was in the White House when his father was shot. On 2 July 1881, when President James A. Garfield was shot by the assassin Charles J. Guiteau at Washington's Baltimore and Potomac Railroad Station, Robert was with him. Finally, on 6 September 1901, when President William McKinley was shot by Leon F. Czolgosz at the Pan American Exposition in Buffalo, Robert was on a train just arriving in Buffalo.

- Several American towns apparently heard reports of Lincoln's assassination before it actually happened. For example, George Kulzer, an inhabitant of Stearns County, Minnesota, told the following story about the town of St Joseph in Minnesota. 'Early in the morning on Wednesday, the fourteenth, people were horror-stricken to hear that President Lincoln had been assassinated. No one knew how the news had arrived, since we had no telegraph. Later we heard that Mr Lincoln had indeed been assassinated, but not until late in the evening of that day.'

— MARIE ANTOINETTE —

Marie Antoinette just did not get it. As the French Revolution raged around her, she was completely unable to comprehend the impact it was having on France and although it is unlikely that she uttered the famous words often attributed to her – 'Let them eat cake!' when people marched in protest at the price of bread – there can be little doubt she would have sympathised with the sentiment.

She was criticised for her extravagant and unconventional lifestyle and was disliked for her opposition to measures designed to ease France's economic difficulties. When things finally began to turn nasty, she and her husband, Louis XVI, tried to flee the country but were caught and arrested. Louis was subsequently tried and executed while Marie Antoinette was imprisoned.

On 12 October 1793, Marie Antoinette underwent a secret preliminary interrogation in the Conciergerie, a prison on the Quai d'Horloge. Once the property of the person in charge of the King of France's residence, it had been a dank, Gothic prison since the late fourteenth century. She was dragged from her bed and led before the young president of the

Revolutionary Tribunal, Martial Joseph Armand Herman, an ally of the dreaded Robespierre. The usual accusations were levelled at her and, as ever, she denied all of the charges.

The Conciergerie was little more than an ante-chamber to the Revolutionary Tribunal which took place in the prison's great chamber. On Monday 14 October she was led through the prison and into the crowded courtroom where her appearance caused a sensation. Contrary to what the spectators had anticipated, the Queen looked haggard – her features were sunken and her hair was white. She was clad in a worn, patched, black dress and swore the oath in the name of Marie Antoinette of Lorraine and Austria, widow of the King of France, born in Vienna. Her armchair was positioned on a platform, so that everyone could see her, although the market-women in the great chamber complained that she should be made to stand so that they could get a better look.

Marie Antoinette answered every question with the words 'I do not believe so,' or 'I don't remember'. But most of what was attested to by the forty witnesses who were called was not much more than gossip. Amongst other things, she was accused of attending orgies, organising feasts, giving money to the Austrian Emperor and encouraging the Swiss Guards to get drunk so that they would go out and massacre French people. She was outraged, however, by accusations that she enjoyed an incestuous relationship with her young son, Louis Charles. Proceedings continued until 11 p.m. that night, with little in the way of evidence being divulged.

Next morning, Marie Antoinette was back in court before she had even had a chance to breakfast. Again the day was spent denying all charges and refuting all of the slurs on her character. By midnight, she had been in court for sixteen hours. After the cross-examination of the fortieth witness, she was asked if she had anything to say. She announced to the court that she was guilty of nothing more than being the King's wife.

She was not present for the summing-up to the jurors by Herman. Anyway, she was convinced that nothing had been proved against her. She believed she would merely be sent into exile. On returning to the courtroom, however, she was horrified to find that she had been found guilty on all counts. The prosecutor asked for the death penalty and, needless to say, it was readily granted. The Queen simply shook her head when she was asked if she had anything to say. She left the courtroom at four in the morning.

Back in her cell, she was given writing materials previously denied to her and wrote a last letter to her sister-in-law. In it she wrote how calm she felt and how clear her conscience was. She regretted only that she was leaving her children. She left a message for her son, Louis Charles – 'Let my son never forget his father's last words … never try to avenge our deaths.'

Rosalie Lamorlière, her servant, came to her cell a few hours later, at 7 a.m. The Queen had eaten nothing for days and even now refused food until she was persuaded to have a few spoonfuls of soup.

Under the gaze of her jailers, she put on a simple white

dress – she had not been allowed to wear her black widow's dress in prison. On her head she put a linen cap with pleated edges to which had been added two streamers and some black crepe, making it into a widow's bonnet. On her legs she wore black silk stockings and on her feet, plum-coloured shoes.

Charles Henri Sanson, the executioner, came to her cell to cut off her hair and her hands were bound while she protested that her husband had not been bound. She had to be untied almost immediately to relieve herself, squatting humiliatingly in a corner of the cell.

Her procession to the scaffold in Place de la Concorde began that morning at eleven o'clock. She rode in a horse-drawn cart, seated with her back to the horses. Huge crowds lined the route and the painter David drew her from a window as she passed while the crowd screamed invective and spat at her.

Arriving at the Place de la Concorde, she stepped down from the cart and is reported to have sprung up the steps to the scaffold, stopping, incredibly, to apologise to her executioner for accidentally stepping on his toes.

Her head was chopped off by Madame Guillotine at 12.15 and held high by Sanson while the crowd rejoiced.

 THE FUNERAL

Marie Antoinette's body was taken to the graveyard off the Rue d'Anjou, where her husband, Louis XVI, had been buried. The gravediggers had lunch before burying her, the head and body lying unattended on the grass. Madame Tussaud sculpted her face in melted wax while she lay there.

☠ POST MORTEM

- Marie Antoinette's last letter never reached her sister-in-law, Madame Elisabeth. It was given instead to Robespierre and only resurfaced in 1816. It is now in the Archives Nationales.
- The few effects of this woman who had once filled the Palace of Versailles with her belongings were distributed to the women of the Saltpêtrière Prison. They consisted of a few linen chemises, corsets in fine toile, a couple of pairs of black stockings, a headdress, some black crepe, a few handkerchiefs, garters and two pairs of cotton pockets in which she carried her belongings. There was also a box of powder, a sponge and a little box of pomade. Four years later an auction was held of other effects found at the Temple – a small green morocco sewing box and three small portraits. They raised ten francs, fifteen centimes.
- News of her death was received joyously throughout France.
- Her son Louis Charles, Louis XVII, died of tuberculosis in 1795, aged ten. There are no direct descendants of Marie Antoinette alive today.
- The remains of Marie Antoinette and Louis were exhumed in 1815 and removed to the cathedral of St Denis, the traditional resting place of the Bourbons.

— MARILYN MONROE —

Marilyn Monroe's death remains one of Tinseltown's greatest mysteries, fuelled by conflicting stories and persistent rumours. Did she take her own life in a haze of pills or was she murdered because she knew enough to ruin reputations at the highest levels?

Sadly, much of the evidence and testimony obtained during the investigation – including police files and interviews – has been lost or destroyed. Therefore, writing about the death of Marilyn can really be only speculative. However, there is certainly a great deal to be speculative about.

Here are just two of many versions of the last hours of the woman who was perhaps Hollywood's greatest star.

VERSION 1

It was Saturday 4 August 1962 and, as usual, Marilyn had not slept well. Pat Newcomb, her press agent, had stayed the night at the house in Brentwood and, waking at noon, found the star to be in a bad mood. 'I had been able to sleep and Marilyn hadn't,' said Newcomb later in an interview. 'When I came out looking refreshed, it made her furious.'

Marilyn spent a large part of the afternoon with her psychiatrist, Dr Ralph Greenson, who had arrived just after lunch, following a phone call from the house asking if there was any oxygen available. She interrupted her consultation only to go for a drive with Eunice Murray, her assistant, who had arrived early that morning and was to spend much of the day there.

By this time it was obvious that Marilyn had swallowed one or more of the Nembutal barbiturate tablets prescribed to her the previous day by Dr Hyman Engelberg. Dr Greenson had been trying to break her Nembutal habit, switching her to other drugs to help her sleep. Nembutal, however, was her drug of choice and she had a number of sources for it as well as a plentiful supply of capsules hidden around the house.

At around 5.30 p.m. Greenson asked Pat Newcomb to leave the house as Marilyn seemed unhappy having her around, speaking sharply to her several times. A little later, at around seven, the doctor also left.

At around 7.15, Marilyn received a phone call from her ex-husband, Joe DiMaggio. He had got engaged but had decided to break off the engagement and wanted to talk to Marilyn about it. He later claimed that she seemed in good spirits when he talked to her, a view confirmed by Eunice Murray. Immediately after the call, Marilyn phoned Dr Greenson to tell him about the broken engagement and he, like the others, thought she sounded fine.

Half an hour later, the actor Peter Lawford called to invite her to a party. But by this time her mood was radically different. She sounded heavily drugged and, he claims, seemed suicidal. He said that he shouted her name into the phone a few times when she didn't respond to his conversation. She is reported to have said, in a line that could have been taken from one of her films, 'Say goodbye to Pat, say goodbye to the president, and say goodbye to yourself, because you're a nice guy.' Lawford panicked and called his friend Milt Ebbins, who, in turn, called Marilyn's lawyer, Milton Rudin. He convinced Rudin that he should go round to her house to check on her condition.

Instead of going to the house, however, Rudin called Eunice at around 8.30, asking her to check on the star. She did so and called back saying Marilyn was fine. Still not satisfied, however, Lawford put in a call at around 11 p.m. to another friend, Joe Naar, who lived close to Marilyn. He agreed to go over to the house to check that she had not overdosed but, just as he was leaving, Rudin called, telling him not to bother. He said that Marilyn had been given a sedative by Dr Greenson.

Eunice woke up around 3 a.m. and claims she saw a light under Marilyn's bedroom door (this claim is suspicious as the carpet's thick pile meant that nothing could be seen under the door). She claimed the door was locked (also suspicious as there was no working lock on the door) and she immediately called Dr Greenson.

Greenson got into Marilyn's room at around 3.50 a.m. and found her dead on her bed.

VERSION 2

Another version of the story places Norman Jeffries, Eunice's son-in-law, at the house that night. According to him, between 9.30 and 10 p.m., the Attorney General, Robert Kennedy, with whom Marilyn had been having an affair, arrived at the house with two other men. They ordered him and Eunice from the house. They went to the house of a neighbour, returning at around 10.30 when Kennedy and the two men left.

Jeffries claims that when they returned to the house, he saw Marilyn lying face down on her bed, naked and holding a telephone. He said she looked dead and Eunice called an ambulance and then the doctor.

Jeffries says that Peter Lawford and Pat Newcomb then arrived at the scene, shocked and hysterical. They summoned help. Ambulance driver Ken Hunter claims to have arrived in the early hours to find her in a coma. She was taken to Santa Monica Hospital where she died. The suggestion is that her body was then returned to her house to facilitate a cover-up.

Another eyewitness account supported Jeffries' claims, but it was never included in the records of the investigation into Marilyn's death. A neighbour told police that she saw Robert Kennedy and the two men approach Marilyn's house at about 6 or 7 p.m., carrying a black medical case. Although police refused to give any credence to her story, it was backed up by several other people who were playing cards with the neighbour. They all say they saw Bobby Kennedy drive up that evening.

Another phone call missing from some accounts is one Marilyn is said to have made to her hairdresser, Sydney Guilaroff, around 8.30 p.m. Guilaroff says that in a rambling conversation, Marilyn claimed to know a lot of dangerous secrets about the Kennedys and in another unrecorded call, to her sometime lover, Jose Bolanos, she is said to have spoken about 'something … that would shock the whole world'. As they spoke, she suddenly put down the phone without hanging up because she thought she had heard a disturbance at her front door. He never heard from her again.

 ## THE FUNERAL

Marilyn's funeral service was held at Westwood Memorial Park, three days after her death. Joe DiMaggio made the arrangements, and only thirty-one close friends and relatives were invited. More than fifty Los Angeles police officers were at the cemetery, assisted by forty security guards hired by Twentieth Century Fox. Stands were set up outside the north wall of the cemetery to accommodate the press, and hundreds of fans stood quietly outside the cemetery gates.

DiMaggio had invited the poet Carl Sandburg to speak at the service, but he was ill and could not attend. The eulogy was delivered by her acting coach, Lee Strasberg. None of Marilyn's co-stars or friends from the entertainment industry was invited, even though many flew to Los Angeles to attend the funeral. 'We could not in conscience ask one personality to attend without perhaps offending many, many others,' DiMaggio said. Privately, however, he blamed the film and entertainment community for his ex-wife's death.

Marilyn was buried in an $800 coffin, wearing a simple chartreuse Pucci dress, with a green scarf tied around her neck. In her hands was a tiny bouquet of baby pink roses, placed there by DiMaggio. After the service, just before the coffin was closed, DiMaggio leant over, kissed Monroe on the lips, and whispered, 'I love you, I love you.' That evening, after the funeral service was completed and Monroe's body had been placed in the crypt, he returned to the cemetery alone for a final, private farewell.

☠ POST MORTEM

- The coroner determined that Marilyn died from an overdose of barbiturates. The drug pentobarbital was found in her liver and chloral hydrate was found in her blood. It was reported that there was no distinguishable physical evidence of foul play. The death was listed as a 'probable suicide'.
- For the next twenty years, until 1983, Joe DiMaggio arranged to have six red roses sent to Marilyn's crypt three times a week. And when DiMaggio himself died in March 1999, his last words were reported to be, 'I'll finally get to see Marilyn.'

- As her body was being prepared at the funeral home, some-one observed that it didn't look like Marilyn Monroe because she was too flat-chested. The autopsy had left her like that but the family had provided a pair of breast-enhancers that Marilyn had worn occasionally. The falsies did not do the job, however, and they were removed from the dress. A version of the most famous chest in the world was created using cotton wool.

 THE CONSPIRACY THEORY

- When Sergeant Jack Clemmons of the West Los Angeles Police Department arrived at the scene of Marilyn's death, at 4.25 p.m., he was led into the bedroom where he found her nude body covered with a sheet. 'She was lying face-down in what I call the soldier's position. Her face was in a pillow, her arms were by her side, her right arm was slightly bent. Her legs were stretched out perfectly straight.' His immediate thought was that she had been placed that way. He had seen a number of suicides and knew that an over-dose of sleeping tablets usually causes victims to suffer con-vulsions and vomiting before they die in a contorted position. He continued: 'Her hands were by her side and her legs were stretched out perfectly straight. It was the most obviously staged death scene I have ever seen. The pill bottles on her bedside table had been arranged in neat order and the body deliberately positioned. It all looked too tidy.'

- The statements of the three who were present seemed unusual to Clemmons. They claimed that Marilyn's body had been discovered some four hours earlier, but that they could not contact the police until Twentieth Century Fox's publicity department had given them permission.

- There was no drinking glass in the bedroom to help Marilyn take the many pills that she was credited with swallowing.

- The attendant who took Marilyn's body to the mortuary, at between 5.30 and 6 a.m. on Sunday morning, noted that 'rigor mortis was advanced', thus placing her time of death at between 9.30 and 11.30 p.m. on Saturday night. Arthur Jacobs, Marilyn's publicist, was informed of Marilyn's death between 10 and 10.30 p.m. on Saturday.

- The conclusions of the autopsy were disputed by some forensic experts who argued that there were no traces of Nembutal in Marilyn's stomach or intestinal tract. Also, there should have been specific crystals and evidence of the yellow capsules in which Nembutal is packaged. Not only were there no capsule parts, there was no yellow dye from the capsules in her stomach. Marilyn's biographer, Donald Spoto, contests that her blood count contained: 'Eight milligrams of chloral hydrate and four and a half milligrams of Nembutal, but in her liver there was a count of thirteen milligrams, a much higher concentration of Nembutal … The ratio of Nembutal found in the blood compared to that in the liver suggested … that Marilyn lived for many hours after the ingestion of that drug … This means that while

Marilyn was alive and mobile throughout the day, the process of metabolising the Nembutal she had taken had reached the liver and was beginning the process of excretion ... The barbiturates were absorbed over a period of not minutes but hours ... This report is consistent with what Greenson himself called her "somewhat drugged" condition.' This would rule out the suspicion of an injection of barbiturates. Plus, there were no needle marks and an injection of such an amount would cause immediate death. The only other way she could have ingested such an amount would be if they were administered in an enema, which would explain the 'abnormal, anomalous discoloration of the colon'. If this was indeed the method, it could only be the result of one of two things – an accident or murder.

- Peter Lawford later claimed that Marilyn was an embarrassment to the Kennedys, especially in her ambitious aspirations to become the First Lady. Their rejection brought an enraged response from Marilyn, hence her claim that she was in possession of information that would shake John Kennedy's presidency. It is very probable that she knew a lot about the president's involvement with Mafia head Sam Giancana and there would, in all likelihood, have been many other indiscretions. Did Bobby Kennedy arrive that night to announce to Marilyn that it was all over?

- FBI tapes made that night are said to record an argument

between Bobby and Marilyn. 'Where is it? Where the fuck is it?' he is reported to be saying and 'My family must have it.' 'We'll make any arrangements you want,' and 'We'll pay you for it.'

- According to author Anthony Summers, Bobby Kennedy would have arrived to find Monroe overdosing but alive. An ambulance was called to take Marilyn to the hospital, but she died en route. Kennedy switched immediately to cover-up mode. According to Summers, the ambulance turned round and returned to the bungalow. The body was laid out on the bed, the room straightened and a call placed to Robert Greenson. It was Greenson who officially discovered the dead Marilyn, by which time Bobby Kennedy was well away. A police officer pulled over a car driven by Peter Lawford sometime after midnight – hours after Marilyn died. Bobby Kennedy was in the back seat.

- One rumour says that she was murdered by the Mafia, in revenge for Robert Kennedy's crusade, as Attorney General, against organised crime.

- Marilyn was an inveterate diary-keeper. Lionel Grandison, of the Los Angeles County Coroner's Office, was the last person to have seen and examined Marilyn's red diary. He had sent his driver to Marilyn's house in the hope of recovering an address book so that relatives could be notified of Marilyn's death but Eunice Murray gave the driver a little red diary as well as an address book. He stated that the diary contained references to the Kennedys and other people (notably Fidel Castro). Before leaving his office for the day, he locked it in the coroner's office safe. When he returned to work on Tuesday 7 August, the safe was still locked but the diary was gone.

— MARY QUEEN OF SCOTS —

By Saturday 4 February 1587, Mary Queen of Scots had been a prisoner for nineteen years. In 1567, deeply unpopular with her nobles and the people of Scotland, she had finally abdicated in favour of her son, James VI, and had crossed the Solway, the river that marked the border between Scotland and England, to seek the protection of the English queen, Elizabeth I. Elizabeth saw her as a threat, however, and, not knowing what to do with her, kept her a permanent prisoner in a succession of English strongholds.

Several plots against Queen Elizabeth had been discovered over the years, none of which seemed to directly involve Mary but one, masterminded by Anthony Babington, had finally implicated her through letters in which she apparently approved Elizabeth's death. As a result, she had been brought to trial in 1586 and sentenced to death. Elizabeth had not signed the death warrant until 1587 but it was by no means certain that she intended it to be carried out.

On that Saturday when Mary's physician, Bourgoing, was given an evasive response to a simple request to go out to neighbouring villages in search of herbal remedies, Mary became suspicious. The arrival on Tuesday 7 February of the earls of Kent and Shrewsbury did little to allay her fears. She began to realise that she would probably have no further need of remedies in this life.

She was given little time to prepare for her death. After dinner that day, the two newly arrived earls and the two custodians of the castle requested a meeting with her. Already in bed, she got up, dressed and received them in her room.

Shrewsbury informed her that she had been condemned to death and the warrant was read out to her. Mary remained calm, replying that she would be happy to shed her blood for her church. She swore on a copy of the New Testament that she was innocent of all the crimes of which she had been found guilty.

Her devout Catholicism meant that she refused the offer of the services of the Protestant Dean of Peterborough to help her prepare for her end and they would not allow her own chaplain to be admitted. The execution, she was told, would take place at eight the following morning.

Her last evening was spent in the company of her servants. She ate a hasty supper and then began to put her affairs in order. She gave each of her servants money and mementoes were put aside for other royals and for her relatives. Then she drew up a will in which she further provided for her servants, named the executors of her estate and asked for requiem Masses to be said in France after her death. She confessed her sins in a letter to her priest, the Chaplain de Préau, and, finally, wrote to her brother-in-law, King Henri of France.

By this time it was two in the morning and she lay down on her bed, fully dressed, her women gathered around her, each dressed in black. As the night echoed to the sound of hammering from the great hall where her scaffold was being erected, one of the servants read from the Bible.

Next day, 8 February, dawned bright and sunny and Mary rose at six to give each of her women a farewell embrace. She then went, alone, to pray and had some bread and wine.

Eventually, sometime between eight and nine, a messenger arrived saying that the lords were ready for her. Mary said goodbye to her servants – Elizabeth had ordered that she had to die alone. After pleading with the lords, however, she was finally permitted to take six of her women into the great hall with her.

The hall was filled with around three hundred spectators, a huge fire blazing in the large fireplace. A wooden stage about twelve feet square and two feet high had been constructed and was hung with black. On the stage there were two stools, one each for Shrewsbury and Kent. Beside them was a small cushioned stool on which the Queen was to sit while her outer garments were being removed. To the side of the stage were more seats for dignitaries and a rank of soldiers. Behind them stood the ordinary people who had been admitted.

Mary entered in silence, dressed entirely in black, except for a long white, lace-edged veil and a white, peaked headdress, also edged with lace. Her satin dress was embroidered with black velvet and had black buttons of jet, trimmed with pearl. Inner sleeves of purple were visible through the slashed sleeves of her dress and contrasting with her shoes of black Spanish leather were stockings decorated with silver. Her garters were of green silk and her petticoat was of crimson velvet. She held a crucifix and a prayer book in her hand and two rosaries dangled from her waist. Her stooping figure had grown full with age.

She was led up the steps to the stage and, still showing no emotion, listened while the warrant for her execution was read out. When the Dean of Peterborough knelt in prayer, Mary turned from him and started to say her own prayer in Latin. When he had finished, she prayed out loud for the Church of England, for her son and for Eizabeth. She kissed the crucifix she held in her hand and ended by asking for her sins to be forgiven.

As was the custom, the executioners asked for forgiveness in advance. Then, helped by two of her servants, they undressed the Queen. She was left wearing a red petticoat and a red bodice, the neckline – considerately for the executioners – cut low at the back. One of her women handed her a pair of red sleeves and she was ready to die, clad entirely in red, the colour of blood and the colour of martyrdom in the Catholic Church.

The executioners stretched out their hands for the Queen's ornaments – a perk of the job – but there were protests when they tried to take her rosary and were told that they would be given money instead.

Her lifelong servant Jane Kennedy bound Mary's eyes with the white cloth embroidered in gold that Mary had chosen, kissing it first and wrapping it around her head like a turban. Only her neck was left bare.

The Queen, still showing no fear, knelt down on the cushion in front of the block, reciting aloud a psalm in Latin. She laid her head on the block, placing her chin carefully with both hands. One of the executioners had to lean forward and move them as they were in the line of the axe's descent. She stretched out her legs and arms and cried out: 'In manus tuas, Domine, confide spiritum meum' ('Into your hands, O Lord, I commend my spirit') three or four times. The assistant to Bull, the executioner, put his hand on her body to steady it for the blow.

Bull missed with his first blow, merely cutting into the back of Mary's head. Her lips moved and her servants reported that they heard her utter the words 'Sweet Jesus'. The next blow severed the neck and it hung by a sinew that was cut using the axe as a saw.

Bull picked the head up and held it aloft, crying out 'God Save the Queen!' Mary's lips were still moving and did so for a quarter of an hour after her death. As he held the head, the auburn tresses came away from it and the head fell to the ground. Her hair underneath was grey and very short.

It was ten o'clock in the morning of Wednesday 8 February. Mary Queen of Scots had died aged forty-four and had chosen to meet her maker wearing a wig.

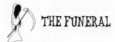 THE FUNERAL

Mary was entombed at Peterborough Cathedral. Elizabeth spent £321 on the funeral to placate Mary's son, King James VI of Scotland.

In 1612, a few years after becoming King of England and Scotland, James had her coffin removed to her final resting place in Westminster Abbey.

 POST MORTEM

- Fearing that relics could be created with them, Mary's heart and other organs were removed and burned that afternoon. Her body was then wrapped in a wax winding sheet and incarcerated in a heavy lead coffin, on Walsingham's explicit orders.

- On being told of the execution, Elizabeth was outraged. She had her secretary, William Davidson, thrown in prison for using the warrant, even though she had signed it. She insisted that she had only signed it 'for safety's sake' and that he was supposed to keep it, not use it. In London, however, bells were rung and there was widespread celebration that the Catholic threat of Mary Queen of Scots had been removed once and for all.

- In France there was an outbreak of national mourning at the news of the dowager Queen's demise and a requiem Mass was held in a black-draped Notre Dame.

- Mary's Skye terrier had been a great comfort to her during the years in prison. It had curled itself around her feet while she knelt at the block and died only a few days after the Queen.
- Meanwhile, Philip of Spain conveniently allowed himself to believe that Mary had disinherited her son James on the eve of her execution and had ceded her claims to the English throne to him. The next year, 1588, he took the momentous decision to pursue his supposed English inheritance with the great force of the Spanish Armada.

— 'AHMAD SHAH MASSOUD —

'Ahmad Shah Massoud has to be considered one of the greatest leaders of guerrilla movements in the twentieth century. He defeated his enemy just like Marshall Tito, Ho Chi Minh and Che Guevara did.' So wrote Robert D. Kaplan in his book *The Soldiers of God*.

Meanwhile, the *Wall Street Journal* called him the 'Afghan who won the cold war', because of the successes he had enjoyed during the Soviet occupation of his country. His troops had been the first Mujahideen group to enter Kabul and he had helped establish a Mujahideen government, in which he served as defence minister. When this government had fallen, the Taliban, with the help of Pakistan, took over the capital and Massoud and his allies had withdrawn to the north of the country, preventing the north and central regions from being taken. During this time, Massoud visited Paris and the European Parliament to urge the world community to put pressure on Pakistan to stop supporting the Taliban and to deliver humanitarian aid to the people of Afghanistan.

On 8 September 2001, a few days before Al-Qaeda's attacks on New York, the 'Lion of Panjshir', as he was known, met with twenty-five of his commanders in the northern Afghan town of Khaja Bahuddin, speaking by telephone to other key figures in the Northern Alliance, the group of warlords he had galvanised against the Taliban.

His discussions finished, at around midnight he summoned his friend of twenty years, Khalili Massoud. As was his habit when he was exhausted and under great pressure, Massoud wanted to talk not about war, but about poetry and Sufi mysticism. Khalili was used to hearing Massoud say: 'Poetry makes me peaceful, it makes me relax.'

Massoud certainly had plenty to worry about. At that time, the Taliban controlled all but ten per cent of the country and a massive attack was expected. Furthermore, the onset of the unforgiving Afghan winter was imminent. The influence of Osama Bin Laden over the Taliban gave him further cause for alarm and persuaded him to ready his troops.

But, on this September night, Massoud pushed all of that to the back of his mind and asked his old friend to read to him from the work of the Persian poet Hafiz. 'Open it; see what will come.' The tradition says that a verse from Iran's most celebrated writer, chosen at random, shows what the future holds.

Khalili read, 'This night we are talking together value it, because many days pass, many months go, many years come, you will not be able to find this night that we are together.'

Massoud had agreed to grant an interview next day to two Arab journalists who had been waiting for two days for their opportunity to meet him. He took Khalili with him as he wanted to accompany him to the Oxus River afterwards for lunch and then travel on to the Panjshir Valley.

They sat in a room of what they called the Afghan Foreign Ministry, Khalili seated to Massoud's right. The cameraman and journalist had introduced themselves as Moroccans – although they were actually Tunisians – representing an Islamic centre based in London and they claimed to have travelled through the Taliban zone. The reporter read out the fifteen questions he wanted to ask. Eight of them referred to Bin Laden and this annoyed Massoud. However, he finally said, 'Okay, is the camera ready?'

'Yes,' said the reporter, calmly and quietly. 'What is the situation in Afghanistan?'

Khalili recalls seeing not the slightest worry in Massoud's eyes, but only the first word was translated when there was a huge explosion. Khalili was seriously hurt, his body riddled by hundreds of splinters, his heart protected by his passport which Massoud had stuffed into his shirt pocket earlier.

Massoud, however, was, in the words of another journalist 'a mess'. His body was taken immediately by helicopter to Tajikistan where he died shortly after.

 THE FUNERAL

Massoud was buried on the hill of Saricha in Panjshir. He had personally selected this place for his grave.

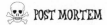 **POST MORTEM**

- Posthumously, the Afghan interim government under President Karzai awarded Massoud the title of Hero of the Afghan Nation.
- Khalili is convinced that Massoud's death was instigated on the orders of Bin Laden who foresaw the consequences of 9/11 – a military campaign that would put an end to the Taliban. He reckons that Massoud's death was designed both to eliminate a potential US ally and to please Mullah Omar, the leader of the Taliban. 'Everyone knows they were sent by Bin Laden,' he says. 'He ordered it personally.'

— MATA HARI —

As was customary, the detachment of soldiers tried to be as noisy as possible as they marched along the corridor to the condemned woman's cell. The intention was to wake her up before their arrival, giving her the first indication that today was the day she would die. The authorities believed it inhumane to announce to the condemned person the date of his or her execution in advance.

But, on this morning – 15 October 1917 – even the stamping of military boots on the hard, cold, stone floor failed to wake Mata Hari, the internationally famous exotic Dutch dancer and courtesan who had been found guilty of spying for Germany and sentenced to death by firing squad. She had taken a sedative the previous evening and its effects had not yet worn off.

She had made a last-minute plea for clemency from the French President, Raymond Poincaré, but as she was gently stirred from her deep sleep by the two nuns who had been attending her and saw her lawyer, Maitre Clunet, and the army captain, Bouchardon, who had interrogated her, she realised that her appeal had been rejected. 'It's not possible!' she exclaimed, becoming overwrought. But the nuns comforted her and she calmed down. 'Don't be afraid, sister,' she said to one in defiance, 'I shall know how to die.'

She asked to write two letters and was immediately provided with ink, pens and stationery. Seated on the edge of her bed, she quickly wrote the letters, sealed them in the envelopes and gave them to her lawyer. She then pulled on a pair of black silk stockings and high-heeled shoes, fastening them with silk ribbons. Over the black silk kimono she was wearing over her nightdress, she placed a long, black, velvet cloak, edged with fur and with a fur collar, wrapping it around her shoulders.

On her head, to cover the braided coils of her black hair, she put a large, black felt hat decorated with a ribbon and a bow. She then pulled on a pair of black kid gloves and said without emotion, 'I am ready.'

A car waited outside the prison to take her to the barracks where the execution was to take place. It was barely 5.30 in the morning and Paris was not yet awake as the vehicle sped along its wide boulevards to the Caserne de Vincennes.

On arriving at their destination, the party quickly descended from the vehicle, Mata Hari getting out last, and walked immediately to the place of execution where twelve soldiers of a Zouave regiment stood at ease. Behind them stood an officer, his sword drawn.

They walked to a mound of earth, seven or eight feet high, that would serve to stop any bullets that were not on target.

A priest, Father Arbaux, spoke quietly to Mata Hari as an officer approached, a white cloth that was to serve as a blindfold fluttering from his hand. He handed it to one of the nuns.

'Must I wear that?' she asked her lawyer. He turned to the officer who replied that she did not have to, if she did not want to. The officer then turned hurriedly away. As the nuns and Maitre Clunet moved away from her, she turned, unbound and un-blindfolded, to look at her executioners. Each looked back, praying that his rifle contained the blank cartridge that had been placed in one of the weapons so that there would always be doubt as to who had actually killed her.

The officer issued a sharp command and the men came to attention. Another command rang out and they raised their rifles to their shoulders, taking careful aim. Mata Hari stood still. The officer moved into view of the firing squad and extended his sword in the air. After the briefest of moments, he dropped it and the soldiers squeezed their triggers, the sound of a dozen gunshots echoing around the barracks.

Mata Hari collapsed slowly to her knees, her head still held up, her expression unchanged. She gazed at the soldiers for a long moment and then slumped backwards, bending at the waist, her legs doubled up beneath her and her face turned towards the sky.

As was customary, one of the officers present walked towards her, drew his pistol and placed the barrel close to her left temple. He pulled the trigger, firing a single bullet into her brain, making sure that the forty-one-year-old woman was dead.

She died as she had lived, however. In the moment before the Zouaves had pulled their triggers, she had blown them a last and memorable kiss.

 ## THE FUNERAL

No one claimed Mata Hari's body. Consequently, she was not afforded the dignity of a funeral. Instead, her body was removed to a medical school where it was dissected to teach medical students.

 ## POST MORTEM

After her death, Mata Hari's fame increased and she became something of a legend. Greta Garbo, Marlene Dietrich, Sylvia Kristel and Jeanne Moreau have all portrayed her on film.

— ERIC MORECAMBE —

In 1984, after years of hard work and a well-publicised series of heart problems, culminating in a triple bypass operation in 1978, Eric Morecambe, half of one of Britain's most successful comedy duos of all time, was looking forward to retirement. His wife Joan recalls in her son Gary's biography of his father that, 'He wanted to spend more time fishing and see much more of his grandchildren. He had an ambition to drive from Boston to Florida, taking in the beauty of Maine and Vermont in the "fall". He wanted to see Rome and Venice. We were ready to relax and enjoy our own company in a way that we had almost never done before.' Further heart worries that year, however, forced him to arrange a return to hospital for more checks. First, though, he had a busy Spring Bank Holiday to enjoy.

He had promised to attend the wedding of a family friend on the Saturday of the holiday weekend and on the Sunday he had agreed to appear at a charity show at the Roses Theatre in Tewkesbury where, in front of an audience, his old friend, the actor and comedian Stan Stennett, would question him about his life and career.

Eric had been put on a course of new pills and they had

eased his discomfort somewhat. Joan recalls that when he awoke on 27 May he was in good spirits, saying that these pills seemed to work and wishing he had been put on them before.

The show was due to start at seven and Eric arrived at the theatre around four in the afternoon. Stan Stennett reported later that he was in great form, cracking jokes with everyone from the cleaners to the stage-hands. He then spent the rest of the time before the show reminiscing about the old days of Variety.

Alan Randall, a musician best known for his uncanny George Formby impersonation that was often seen on television at the time, spent some time in Eric's company prior to the show. He said that Eric was excited to be returning to the theatre and said how much more relaxing it was than television.

He gave a characteristically wonderful performance, talking about his childhood, his first music and dance lessons, his mother Sadie, his work in the mines as a Bevan Boy, his first meeting with his comedy partner Ernie Wise and their climb to the very pinnacle of their profession. He even made jokes about his open-heart surgery. The audience was in stitches.

At the end of the show, the musicians came back on and picked up their instruments. To the audience's delight Eric emerged from the wings and joined them, playing the vibraphone, the sticks flying out of his hands into the front stalls. He then did his famous out-of-tune piano routine.

His wife, Joan, however, was worried that he might tire himself out. But, finally, to her great relief, after his sixth curtain call, he said 'That's your lot!' and walked offstage. But, as he reached the wings, he seemed to catch his breath and suddenly collapsed, hitting his head as he fell. The curtains were lowered immediately and someone rushed onto the stage to ask if there was a doctor in the house.

Joan, her heart sinking, hurried backstage where she found her husband stretched out on the floor. The mayor of Tewkesbury, who was in the audience, was a doctor and he began to give Eric the kiss of life, succeeding in getting his heart beating again.

An ambulance rushed him to the intensive care unit at Cheltenham General Hospital where Joan was allowed to sit with him. He was still unconscious, but seemed to be trying to wake up. To try to wake him, a nurse told Joan to speak loudly to him. They both called his name and as they did so, Joan felt his hand clench hers. Suddenly, she was filled with hope.

As they continued to treat him, she waited in a side room. After about fifteen minutes, however, a doctor emerged to give her the sad news that her husband's heart had finally stopped.

Shortly before four o'clock on the morning of Monday 28 May, Eric Morecambe, Britain's best-loved comedian, was pronounced dead at the age of fifty-eight.

 THE FUNERAL

Eric's funeral took place at the Church of St Nicholas, Harpenden. More than a thousand people attended and the service was relayed by loudspeakers to the crowd outside.

Ernie Wise tearfully read out the lyrics of the duo's signature song *Bring Me Sunshine* and the principal address was delivered by comedian Dickie Henderson whom Morecambe had 'booked' specifically for the task after hearing him speak the year before at a memorial service for Arthur Askey. He had written to Henderson:

> Stalag 13
> Harpenden
> East Berlin

Dear Dickie

I very rarely write to famous people ... that's why I'm writing to you.

I would just like to say that I thought you were superb the other day and I am sure that Big Arthur would have been proud of you. You made us all realise what a great loss we have suffered and at the same time you made us all happy. I would like to book you for mine ... work permitting.

I would like to be cremated and my favourite music is *Smoke Gets in Your Eyes*.

Okay, that's fixed.

Love

Eric

PS I'll pay you when I see you down there. Nothing in this letter constitutes a contract.

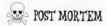 **POST MORTEM**

- Ernie Wise died on 21 March 1999, aged seventy-three.
- In 1999, the town of Morecambe commissioned sculptor Graham Ibbeson to create a larger-than-life statue of Eric Morecambe. It was unveiled by the Queen and has become one of the most visited attractions in the north-west of England.
- A British internet poll in 1999 voted Morecambe the funniest person of the twentieth century.

CAPTAIN LAWRENCE 'TITUS' OATES

Lawrence Oates was born into a life of wealth and privilege. As was customary for a member of his class, he went to Eton and, leaving university, became a professional soldier, holding a commission in the Eniskillen Dragoons, an elite cavalry regiment. His bravery in the Boer War led to him being recommended for the Victoria Cross.

After the war, however, he became increasingly disenchanted with the army. Hearing, while stationed in India in 1909, of Captain Robert Falcon Scott's plans to mount an expedition to reach the South Pole, he decided to pay out of his own pocket the £1,000 – no small sum in those days – it would take to get out of the army.

Oates should probably never have been anywhere near an expedition involving a 1,800 mile walk across Antarctica's frozen wastes, hauling sledges. He had been shot during the Boer War and had been left with one leg two inches shorter than the other, giving him a noticeable limp. He was also an outsider in the group – a soldier amongst sailors.

However, the stiff upper lip of his upbringing and the British tradition of self-sacrifice overrode everything, down to his concealment of his severely frostbitten and gangrenous feet as they marched across the ice.

He was key to the expedition due to his ability to handle horses and horses were essential to the first four hundred miles of the trek. However, he began to see how chaotic Scott's leadership could be when Cecil Meares, who knew nothing about horses, was sent to buy the animals. Oates was horrified by what Meares brought back.

During the march Oates clashed frequently with Scott. He wrote at one point: 'Myself, I dislike Scott intensely and would chuck the whole thing if it were not that we are a British expedition ... he is not straight, it is himself first, the rest nowhere.' He was particularly upset at what he saw as Scott's mismanagement, praising Roald Amundsen, who had reached the Pole a month before the British expedition using dogs instead of men to haul the heavy sledges.

A fundamental disagreement existed between the two men about the way the horses should be used. It was Oates' opinion that they should be driven into the ground and then shot to provide food, but this made Scott squeamish and he rejected the idea, a decision they would all live to regret.

When they were positioning the '100 Ton' depot – vital in providing them with supplies on their return from the Pole – Scott decided to place it thirty miles further north than planned. Oates warned him that he would regret not positioning it thirty miles further south. That thirty miles was to prove crucial as they battled their way back from the Pole in horrific conditions.

Ironically, it was at that spot eighteen weeks later, after arriving at the Pole on 17 January that Oates' suffering became too much. He could walk only with great difficulty; his feet were black and swollen – the result of severe frostbite and gangrene. The side-effects of scurvy had reopened his old war wound and it was turning septic. Like the others, he was suffering from malnutrition.

Day after day, he had struggled on and on, finally unable to haul his sledge and on the night of 15 March when he lay down he hoped he would not wake up. But he did wake. His companions would not leave him to perish, but he knew provisions and fuel were very short, and to wait together only meant that they would die together.

Therefore, on the morning of 16 March 1912, the day before his thirty-second birthday, Lawrence 'Titus' Oates crawled from the tent out into temperatures of minus forty degrees, uttering his famous parting shot: 'I am just going outside and may be some time.'

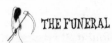 THE FUNERAL

When the bodies of Scott, Wilson and Bowers were found and buried eight months later, the search party searched for twenty miles to the south, trying to find Lawrence Oates' body. They were unsuccessful, however and, instead, built a cairn to his memory.

💀 POST MORTEM

- Oates' sacrifice was in vain. After struggling on until 29 March Captain Scott, Dr Wilson and Lieutenant Bowers perished in their tent, only eleven miles from One Ton depot, where lay a ton of food and fuel specially prepared for their use.

- When news got back to Britain of the tragedy, Oates became an instant hero. 'He laid down his life for others' was a typical newspaper headline.

- Oates died not realising that he was a father. A little girl, who was born at an unknown location in Ireland, was taken from her young mother and sent to an orphanage in the south of England and grew up not knowing her father's identity. Oates was unaware of the child, and the dark secret remained untold for nearly a hundred years. The mother of the child was only twelve years of age when she gave birth. Her family, who came from Scotland, sent the pregnant girl to Ireland to have the child in secrecy.

- At the Oates family home in Gestingthorpe, Essex, a memorial plaque was installed in the local church by the officers of the Enniskillen Dragoons. Oates' mother polished the plaque every week until she died.

- The Enniskillen Dragoons, in their current guise as the Royal Dragoon Guards, now regard him as the greatest hero of their regiment. They celebrate his memory with a service in St Mary the Virgin Church, Gestingthorpe, and a parade for old comrades every year on the Sunday nearest to 16 March.

— GEORGE ORWELL —

In January 1950, University College Hospital played host to a procession of illustrious visitors – the poet Stephen Spender, novelist Anthony Powell, broadcaster and writer Malcolm Muggeridge and representatives of the BBC and left-wing newspapers and periodicals amongst them. They were visiting the writer George Orwell. The most regular visitor was Orwell's new wife, Sonia Brownell, his second wife and sixteen years his junior whom he had met when she worked on Cyril Connolly's monthly magazine, *Horizon*. Her previous lovers read like a *Who's Who* of the contemporary cultural landscape, including the artists Lucien Freud and William Coldstream.

The pair had been married by special licence in Orwell's hospital room on 13 October 1949. David Astor, proprietor of the *Observer*, had been best man and in attendance were a friend of Sonia's parents, the hospital chaplain, Powell, Muggeridge and one of Orwell's doctors. The guests had then enjoyed a celebratory dinner at the Ritz while the bridegroom remained in bed. While the marriage was a puzzle to a number of Orwell's friends – there were accusations of gold-digging and a rumour that Sonia married him because Cyril Connolly had told her to – there was little doubt that it raised the ailing writer's spirits.

George Orwell had been at UCH for four months but, all told, had been in hospital since the start of the previous year. He had finally been diagnosed with tuberculosis after suffering with chronic lung problems for nearly twenty years. The previous summer, he had come close to death at a Gloucestershire sanatorium but had recovered sufficiently to be moved to London where he would come under the care of the distinguished chest specialist Andrew Morland, who had been recommended to Orwell by his publisher, Fred Warburg. While Morland was dismissive of any thought of a cure, he was certain that he could help Orwell live a bearable, if sedentary life. Orwell, for his part, was desperate to return to writing.

He was a private patient. He could afford it. His novel *Nineteen Eighty-Four* had been published to acclaim on both sides of the Atlantic the previous June and twenty-five thousand copies had already been sold in Britain alone. In America its sales had been helped by its selection as a *Book of the Month Club* choice and royalties were rolling in.

He was, however, very unwell and so thin that the doctors found it difficult to insert needles into his body. It was planned that when he was well enough, he would be sent to a Swiss sanatorium, but he had been showing little sign of improvement. Streptomycin, the latest American wonderdrug, had been tried, but its horrific side effects included Orwell's fingernails falling out. Fred Warburg had pleaded with Orwell's US publishers to speed up the delivery of another drug, auromycin, but to no avail.

As his condition grew worse, Orwell hatched plans for further books – a study of Conrad's political fiction and a novella set in the Far East with the working title *A Smoking-Room Story*.

Morland believed that the prospect of the Swiss trip would have a positive effect and, consequently, he sanctioned it for January. At the foot of Orwell's bed sat a fishing rod, bought for him by a friend to be used during his convalescence. However, few of his visitors believed he would live long enough to use it.

Meanwhile, as time wore on, his condition deteriorated. Muggeridge and Powell visited on Christmas Day and described him as 'very deathly and wretched, alone, with Christmas decorations all around'. Muggeridge recorded that his face looked practically dead and oddly resembled a picture he had once seen of Nietzsche on his deathbed. They discussed Orwell's adventures in the Home Guard and his time in Spain during the Spanish Civil War and 'all the while' Muggeridge wrote later, 'the stench of death was in the air, like autumn in a garden'.

They had set 25 January as the date on which he would be leaving for Switzerland on a privately chartered plane. Travelling with him would be Sonia and Lucien Freud. However, when Muggeridge visited him again on the twelfth, he thought he looked worse than ever and he found him miserable and complaining that the doctors would not even let him have an aspirin. A week later, though, he seemed to have picked up, talking enthusiastically to Julian Symons about the trip and his writing.

Sonia spent the night of Friday 21 January at a nightclub with Lucien Freud and it was not until the early hours of Saturday morning that she was tracked down and told by telephone that Orwell had suffered a massive lung haemorrhage and had died.

 ## THE FUNERAL

Orwell had stipulated that he should be buried according to the rites of the Church of England and his body interred (not cremated) in the nearest convenient cemetery. The task of arranging this fell to Powell and Muggeridge and a Warren Street undertaker was quickly brought on board. With David Astor's influence, a plot was secured in the graveyard of All Saints Church at Sutton Courteney in Oxfordshire. Muggeridge noted in his diary that Orwell died on Lenin's birthday and was being buried by the Astors, 'which seems to me to cover the full range of his life'.

The funeral took place on Thursday 26 January. The evening before, Powell and his wife, Lady Violet, called in at the Muggeridges after supper, bringing Sonia with them, 'obviously in a poor way'. On their last meeting, the day after Orwell's death, Sonia had been overcome with grief and

Muggeridge decided that he would 'always love her for her true tears'. He gives a detailed account of the next day's events: Fred Warburg greeting the mourners at the church door, the chilly atmosphere, the congregation 'largely Jewish and almost entirely unbelievers' who had difficulty following the Anglican liturgy. Powell chose the hymns – 'All People That On Earth Do Dwell', 'Guide Me, O Thou Great Redeemer' and 'Ten Thousand Times Ten Thousand' ('Why, I can't remember,' Powell later wrote. 'Perhaps Orwell himself had talked of the hymn, or because he was, in his way, a sort of saint, even if not one in sparkling raiment bright').

Both Powell and Muggeridge found the occasion very distressing. Muggeridge, in particular, was deeply moved by the lesson, chosen by Powell from Ecclesiastes: 'Then shall the dust return to the earth as it was, and the spirit shall return to the God who gave it.' He went back to his house near Regent's Park to read through the sheaf of obituaries filed by, among others, Symons, V. S. Pritchett and Arthur Koestler, seeing in them already 'how the legend of a human being is created'.

 POST MORTEM

- In the last month of his life, the value of George Orwell's estate was put at around £12,000 (the average weekly wage was well below £10).
- Orwell had made a will three days before his death, in the

presence of Sonia and his first wife's sister, Gwen O'Shaughnessy. It transferred his literary estate to Sonia. A substantial life insurance policy would provide for his adopted son Richard, then being looked after by his aunt, Orwell's sister Avril.

— EVA PERÓN —

Eva Perón had been ill since 1950. A few days after she had fainted while inaugurating a building in Buenos Aires, they had removed her appendix, but also discovered the real cause of her constant exhaustion and ill health – cancer of the uterus, ominously the disease that had killed the first wife of her husband, Argentinean President Juan Domingo Perón.

Now, two years later, she lay in a room in the Presidential residence that was far enough away from his room to prevent him hearing her screams, waiting to die.

She had been born into poverty on 7 May 1919, as Eva Duarte, and her parents had never married. By the age of twenty she had moved to Buenos Aires and had begun to find success as an actress in films and on radio.

In 1944, she met Colonel Juan Perón for the first time. He was working in the Argentinean Labour Department and was twenty-seven years older than her, but age did not deter them. Before long they had scandalised Buenos Aires society by moving in together. In 1946, he was elected President of Argentina, with Eva campaigning resolutely at his side. People, especially the poor, loved her passion and began to call her Evita, 'Little Eva'.

She created the Eva Perón Foundation, having diverted government funding for it from another organisation, the Sociedad de Beneficencia, a group of well-to-do ladies who had unwisely snubbed her because of her humble origins. In the next few years she spent tens of millions of dollars helping the poor, building hospitals, schools and old people's homes. She campaigned for and got the vote for Argentinean women and became idolised in her country.

In August 1951, Juan and Evita climbed onto a stage in Buenos Aires to be greeted by the hysterical demands of the huge crowd for Evita to stand as vice-president in the forthcoming presidential elections. In a magnificent piece of theatre, she agreed to comply with the will of the people. The military had other ideas, however, and bridled at the thought of a woman vice-president who would be just a heart attack away from taking over from her husband and assuming command of the armed forces. Nine days after she had responded to the crowd's pleas, she withdrew her candidacy, fearing a military coup.

On 17 October, an assembly was held to celebrate Evita's renunciation of her candidacy. Her husband delivered a eulogy to her and then she delivered a speech containing words that resonated with the Argentinean people – 'I have left the shreds of my life on the road.' On its conclusion, she collapsed into Juan's arms.

In September she was examined under general anaesthetic at the President Perón Clinic, a facility built by her foundation.

The surgeon was George Pack from the Memorial Cancer Center in NewYork, but Evita was not told who he was or what her illness was. It was decided that she required a hysterectomy and in early November Pack returned to carry out the procedure. Meanwhile, they hid from the outside world the true nature of her illness.

They removed her uterus and some lymph nodes, but discovered with dismay that the cancer had spread. Still, the prognosis following the operation was positive. A few days later, when the election took place, the first in which Argentine women could exercise their right to vote, a ballot box was brought to her bedside. A photograph at the time shows her to be frail and thin. The writer David Viñas related how as he took the ballot box containing her vote back to the polling station, a woman knelt before him on the pavement and kissed it.

Inevitably, Perón won with a landslide and by Christmas, Eva was beginning to return to public life, giving a talk on the radio and distributing Christmas presents to poor children who had been brought to the residence. She began to meet with workers and ministers, but by February 1952, she was unwell again, the pain of her cancer returning and her weight loss becoming dramatic. Another biopsy revealed the further spread of the disease. They calculated that she had no more than a month to live.

She was stronger than they thought, however. In early April she attended the funeral of the man who had replaced her as vice-presidential candidate, Hortensio Quijano, and next day she read the manuscript of her autobiography. That same day, Prince Bernard of the Netherlands awarded her the Great Cross of the Orange-Nassau Order.

On 1 May, she made her final speech. She was skeletal, but wearing a shapeless dress to disguise it. Juan held her up by the waist as the cheers of the huge crowd resounded around the square.

On 4 June she was still alive but weighed only eighty-two pounds and could barely stand. When Perón travelled to the Argentinean Congress building, standing up and waving in an open-topped car, she stood beside him. But a huge dose of morphine coursed through her veins and her fur coat hid a belt that lashed her to the window behind the driver. They had also created a plaster support for her. Through it all, she waved and smiled.

The country held Masses for her, broadcast on national radio, but she was not allowed to listen as they persisted in lying to her about her condition. The newspapers she read were specially printed editions that excluded all mention of her illness. Family and friends stayed with her in eight-hour shifts.

On 18 June, she slipped into a coma. Once again, the doctors wrote her off, but once again she awoke and, saying that she would die if she stayed in bed, incredibly, she got up.

On the night before she died, Perón visited her. He had had great trouble accepting what his once-beautiful wife had become in illness and had not been to see her for two days.

Next day, Saturday 26 July, when her mother, Doña Juana, briefly left her room, Evita sighed to her sister Elisa, 'Poor old lady.' Elisa replied that, on the contrary, their mother looked good. Evita replied: 'I know. *Lo Digo porque Eva se va*' ('I say this because Eva is leaving)'. They were the last words she would utter.

She died, aged thirty-three.

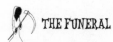

THE FUNERAL

There would be no funeral for Evita for a while.

POST MORTEM

- Spanish doctor Pedro Ara had been engaged to mummify Evita's corpse. He went to work immediately, making her first of all look good for her lying in state at the Ministry of Labour. Her hair was coloured and styled in her customary chignon and her nails were manicured. Dressed in a white shroud and the Argentine flag, she was placed in a glass casket, rosary beads, given to her by the Pope, interwoven in her fingers. Queues formed, stretching for miles, and two people died as they waited in the rain. For thirteen days they queued to touch or kiss the casket. For three of those days the entire country had to wear a black tie or armband. On 9 August, she was borne on a gun carriage in front of an audience of two million on the wet streets of the capital to

Congress and then to the building of the Argentinean labour confederation to await the construction of a huge monument that Juan had planned. There, Pedro Ara began his work, preserving her body for all time, as a kind of metaphor for Perónism.

- The monument failed to materialise but it became immaterial when, in September 1955, Perón was overthrown and was forced into exile in Madrid, leaving Evita's preserved body behind. For a while, she remained with Ara before being taken by the army. She was supposed to be buried in a local cemetery, but the officer in charge of her corpse kept her. Rediscovered, she was taken secretly to Italy, where she was buried with another woman's name on the headstone in a cemetery in Milan. A letter containing details of her location was given to new president Pedro Aramburu, but he refused to open it, giving it to a lawyer and ordering him to pass it to the next president four weeks after his death.

- In 1970 former President Aramburu was taken from his home by two men in uniform and questioned about many things including the location of Eva Perón's body. He told them only that the Vatican had supervised her burial and lied that she was in Rome. He would say no more and for his obduracy he was executed. Four weeks after his death, the lawyer passed the letter to General Alexandro Lanusse, head of the Argentine government of the time.

- Her body was discovered in Milan and transported by road to Spain. She was delivered to Perón in Madrid in the back of a bakery truck and he kept her in the attic of his home.
- The body was still in an astonishingly good condition, but there was some damage to her nose and feet as well as gashes on her cheek. A finger was missing.
- In October 1973, Perón was miraculously returned to power on a wave of Perónist nostalgia. He had remarried and his new wife, Isabel, appeared on posters with him. But there was a third person on those posters and billboards – Evita. He lasted only nine months, however, before dying of a heart attack. Isabel took over the presidential reins.
- On 17 November 1974, Eva Perón's body finally returned to Argentina. She was taken to Juan's Olivos residence and repair work was undertaken.
- On 26 March 1976, during the overthrow of Isabel Perón by a military coup led by future president General Videla, Evita's body was ejected from the Olivos residence. In October of that year, the casket was returned to her family and she was finally laid to rest in the family vault in Buenos Aires' Recoleta Cemetery, twenty-four years after her death.

— RIVER PHOENIX —

The 30 October 1993 was just another day for handsome young film star River Phoenix. He spent much of it in front of the camera on a Hollywood sound stage, filming interior scenes for *Dark Blood*, in which he was playing a hermit living on a nuclear testing site, waiting for the end of the world. *Dark Blood* had marked a return to acting for Phoenix. A few years previously, he had become tired of the star machine, returning to live with his family in Florida and calling himself Rio. Now his career was back on track and he had just signed to star in a major production, *Interview with a Vampire*, alongside Tom Cruise.

When the cameras stopped rolling at around 7 p.m., River returned to his hotel, the Nikko. Waiting for him there were his actress girlfriend Samantha Mathis, his sister Rain and brother Joaquin. Before long the quartet were partying noisily. However, River was set that evening on heading to the Viper Room at 8852 Sunset Boulevard, an infamous club frequented by celebrities and part-owned by another rising young film star, Johnny Depp. Even in the 1940s, the Viper Room had enjoyed a dubious reputation. As the Melody

Room, it had been used by gangster Bugsy Siegel as an illicit gambling den.

Some friends of River were playing at the Viper Room that night – Flea from Red Hot Chili Peppers, AJ of the band Ministry and Gibby Haynes of the Butthole Surfers. So, at around 10 p.m. the group left the Nikko and travelled to the club by car, River wearing a pair of striped brown trousers and black and white Converse high tops.

At 1 a.m., he was in the bathroom doing drugs with some drug-dealer friends when someone offered him a snort of high-grade Persian Brown, telling him it would make him feel fabulous. Immediately after snorting the drug, however, River began trembling and shaking uncontrollably. He screamed at his friend and vomited. Incredibly, someone tried to help by giving him a Valium.

The young actor staggered back out into the bar looking for Samantha Mathis and Rain Phoenix. By this time, he was having difficulty breathing and briefly passed out. Coming round, he asked Mathis to take him outside for some air. Mathis and Joaquin helped him out but he collapsed on the pavement and began having seizures.

Ron Davis, a photographer waiting outside the club for celebrity photo opportunities, called 911 at the nearby pay-phone, as did Joaquin. When Rain Phoenix emerged from the Viper Room, she threw herself on River in a vain attempt to stop the seizures. Suddenly, however, he stopped moving and became very still. He had stopped breathing. It was 1.14 a.m.

Paramedics arrived to find him in full cardiac arrest and Ray Ribar of the LA County Fire Department began to administer heart massage. The actor was put in the ambulance and rushed to Cedars Sinai Medical Centre, being admitted at 1.34 a.m.

By the time of his arrival, River's skin was dark blue, but his body was still warm. For twenty frantic minutes, doctors fought to revive him, even inserting a pacemaker. It was all futile. At 1.51 a.m. on 31 October 1993, River Phoenix was pronounced dead, aged just twenty-three.

 ## THE FUNERAL

River was placed in a blue coffin for a viewing on 4 November at the Milam Funeral Home. He was wearing a black t-shirt with the logo of his band, Aleka's Attic, on it and his normally blonde shoulder-length hair, dyed black for *Dark Blood*, had been cut by the mortician. At the request of Heart Phoenix, River's mother, the shorn hair was placed beside him in the coffin. Heart placed a single carnation in the casket and many of the sixty mourners also left items such as notes and necklaces.

After his cremation, his ashes remained in the care of his family. A memorial service, held on the Paramount Studios lot on 18 November, was attended by Sidney Poitier, Rob Reiner, Richard Benjamin, John Boorman and Peter Bogdanovich.

💀 POST MORTEM

- The official cause of River Phoenix's death was acute multiple drug ingestion. The autopsy showed lethal levels of cocaine and morphine (heroin shows up as morphine, as the body metabolises it), Valium, marijuana and ephedrine. Ephedrine is the main ingredient found in crystal meth.

- The telephone call made by Joaquin Phoenix, calling the emergency services, was aired repeatedly in the media over the days following his brother's death. 'You must get here, please, because he's dying,' he is heard screaming in desperation.

— PABLO PICASSO —

'Death holds no fear for me,' Pablo Diego José Francisco de Paula Juan Nepomuceno María de los Remedios Cipriano de la Santísima Trinidad Martyr Patricio Clito Ruíz y Picasso – aka Pablo Picasso – once told a friend. 'It has a kind of beauty. What I am afraid of is falling ill and not being able to work. That's lost time.'

On 7 April 1973, Picasso was, as usual, losing no time. Despite having been laid low with a bad bout of influenza the previous winter, the ninety-one-year-old artist was hard at it in Notre-Dame-de-Vie, his hilltop villa at Mougins on the French Riviera, preparing for the following month's exhibition in Avignon of two hundred examples of his recent work. Of course, Picasso no longer had any need for money or the blandishments of critics. These days, he was in competition only with himself and the great works of his life.

In the late afternoon sunshine, he went for a stroll in the little park surrounding the sprawling stone house with its view of the foothills of the Maritime Alps. There, he would often gather flowers and vegetables and take them into his studio to draw them. Jacques Barra, Picasso's gardener, recalls: 'That day I showed him the anemones and pansies, which he particularly liked.'

In the evening, Picasso and his wife, Jacqueline, entertained some friends for dinner, Picasso, in high spirits, urging the guests to 'Drink to me; drink to my health! You know I can't drink any more.'

At 11.30, he rose from the table, announcing that he had to go back to work. He remained in his studio, painting until 3 a.m.

Next day, Sunday 8 April, Picasso woke, as usual, at 11.30, but was unable to get out of bed. Jacqueline and his son, Paolo, immediately summoned help, but, just ten minutes later, before a doctor could get there, the twentieth century's greatest artist had a heart attack and died.

 THE FUNERAL

Picasso was interred at Castle Vauvenargues' park, in Vauvenargues, Bouches-du-Rhône. Jacqueline prevented his children Claude and Paloma from attending the funeral.

 POST MORTEM

- Picasso's death was attributed to a heart attack brought on by pulmonary oedema, fluid in the lungs.
- At the time of his death, by now a multi-millionaire, he owned a vast quantity of his own work, consisting of

personal favourites that he had kept off the art market. He also had a considerable collection of the work of many other famous artists, such as Henri Matisse, with whom he had exchanged works. Since he had left no will, his death duties were paid in kind, in the form of works by him and others from his collection. These constitute the core of the immense and representative collection at the Musée Picasso in Paris.

- In 2003, his relatives inaugurated a museum dedicated to him in his birthplace, Malaga – the Museo Picasso Malaga.
- Jacqueline Roque, Picasso's second wife, shot herself thirteen years after Picasso's death.

— SYLVIA PLATH —

As 1962 faded into 1963, Britain seemed to be covered by a sheet of ice. It was the worst winter for sixty years and thirty-year-old Sylvia Plath and her children, Frieda and Nicholas, had been suffering from flu. Living in a second-floor flat at 23 Fitzroy Road, Primrose Hill, Sylvia was experiencing violent mood swings and was undergoing treatment for depression. She was struggling to cope and had hired a Belgian au pair, but the girl had lasted less than a month.

At the end of the first week of February Sylvia's doctor, Dr Horder, was becoming concerned. She was thin and anxious and her sleeping pills were no longer working. Additionally, her depression was not being eased by the new medication he had prescribed. He tried unsuccessfully to find a hospital bed for her for the weekend but she ended up at a friend's house, railing against her estranged husband, the poet Ted Hughes, for his infidelity and depressed by the indifference of American reviewers to her novel *The Bell Jar*.

She returned home on 10 February claiming that she was feeling better. But when she went down to the flat of a neighbour at 11.45 that night to buy some stamps from him he thought she looked very ill and suggested calling a doctor. She refused and they said goodnight. Ten minutes after he had closed the door, however, he opened it again to find Sylvia still standing there. Again she refused his pleas to contact her doctor, telling him that she was having a vision or a dream. For the rest of the night he heard her pacing the floor above his head.

Sometime early in the morning of 11 February Sylvia made careful preparations. She placed bread and cups of milk beside her children's beds, opened their windows wide and stuffed the cracks in the bedroom and kitchen doors with towels. She had already consumed a quantity of sleeping pills and had written a note asking that her doctor be called.

Around nine, a nurse who visited her daily became concerned that her knocks at the door were going unanswered. She found a builder who gained entrance and in the kitchen, they found Sylvia's body. She had knelt beside the open gas oven and turned on the gas.

She had attempted suicide once before, while attending Smith College in her home town of Boston.

This time it worked.

 ## THE FUNERAL

Sylvia Plath was buried on 16 February 1963, in Heptonstall Cemetery, West Yorkshire, close to the Hughes family home, under the name 'Sylvia Plath Hughes'. The inscription reads: 'Even amidst fierce flames/The golden lotus can be planted'.

☠ POST MORTEM

- On 17 February 1963, in the *Observer* newspaper, the critic Al Alvarez wrote a memorial essay about Plath, *A Poet's Epitath*, in which he eulogised: 'The loss to literature is inestimable.'
- In 1965, *Ariel*, the collection of the forty poems she had written in the months before her death, was published. By 1968, more than eight thousand hardbacks and twenty thousand paperbacks had been sold in the UK alone. Further collections followed in coming years and all sold phenomenally well.
- Six years after Sylvia's death, Assia Wevill, the woman who had lured Ted Hughes away from Plath, killed herself and their four-year-old daughter Shura in exactly the same way that Sylvia did.
- Hughes was vilified for years after Sylvia's suicide, especially by feminists. Often, his readings were disrupted by women bearing banners declaring him a murderer.
- The name 'Hughes' has on many occasions been scratched off Sylvia's tombstone.

⟜ EDGAR ALLAN POE ⟜

The misery of Edgar Allan Poe's life is matched only by the mystery of his death.

His young wife, Virginia, whom he had married in 1835 when she was only thirteen, had died of tuberculosis in the early 1840s and Poe had become increasingly unstable. Although he had achieved a measure of success with his poem 'The Raven', published in 1845, it had failed to make him rich – he had earned a paltry $9 from its publication. The precarious nature of his professional life as a writer and magazine editor coupled with the stress of Virginia's illness and early death had increased his already heavy drinking.

Poe had been living in a cottage in the Bronx and had become engaged to the poet, essayist and spirtualist Sarah Helen Whitman. But she began to tire of his erratic behaviour and frequent drunkenness. In 1848, for instance, when he was travelling to visit Sarah in Providence, he took an overdose of laudanum and almost died. He eventually took a vow to remain sober during their engagement, but no sooner had he taken the vow than it had been broken. To make matters worse, Sarah's mother was set against him marrying her daughter and she accused him of pursuing two other women while engaged to her daughter. The relationship ended.

He had been in Richmond, Virginia, visiting Sarah Elmira Royster, a former childhood sweetheart with whom he was attempting to rekindle a relationship, and on 27 September, he took a train from Richmond to New York. No more was heard of him until 3 October when a printer by the name of Joseph W. Walker found him seated on a wooden plank outside Ryan's Tavern on Lombard Street in Baltimore. Poe was delirious, unwashed and shabbily dressed, uncharacteristic for a man normally punctilious about his appearance. The doctor who attended him, John Joseph Moran, later said he was wearing a stained and faded woollen jacket, dirty trousers, an old straw hat and a pair of down-at-heel worn-out shoes.

The writer was conveyed in a carriage to Washington College Hospital, Baltimore, where he was put in a wing of the hospital with bars on the windows, reserved for people who were ill from drinking, although Moran quickly realised that Poe was not drunk. But he was incoherent for much of the time, uttering the name 'Reynolds' repeatedly. He was unable in his delirium to say how he came to be in this state on a street in Baltimore, apparently dressed in someone else's clothes, and Dr Moran surmised that he had been robbed and his clothing had been stolen.

When asked about his friends, Moran claims that Poe said: 'My best friend would be the man who gave me a pistol that I might blow out my brains.' He referred to a wife, possibly forgetting in his feverish condition that Virginia was dead.

At five in the morning of 7 October, Edgar Allan Poe is said to have uttered the words: 'Lord help my poor soul' and died, aged forty.

 ## THE FUNERAL

Poe was buried on the grounds of Westminster Hall and Burial Ground in a simple ceremony at 4 p.m. on Monday 8 October 1849, in a cheap mahogany coffin paid for by his uncle, Henry Herring. It lacked handles, a nameplate, a cloth lining and a cushion for his head. The hearse was paid for by his cousin, Neilson Poe, and his shroud was made by the wife of Dr Moran.

In attendance were Poe's friend Dr Joseph Snodgrass, a former University of Virginia classmate, and his cousin Elizabeth Herring and her husband. It was a damp, bitter cold day and the Reverend W. T. D. Clemm, a cousin of Poe's late wife, decided to dispense with a sermon in view of the cold and the small number of mourners. The proceedings lasted a mere three minutes.

 ## POST MORTEM

- A white, Italian marble headstone planned for the grave and paid for by Neilson Poe was destroyed when a train derailed and crashed into the yard where it was being stored. Consequently, his grave was marked by a piece of sandstone on which was inscribed 'No. 80'. In 1873, however, following a visit to Poe's grave, the poet Paul Hamilton Hayne wrote a newspaper article suggesting a better monument. Money was raised in Baltimore and throughout the United States and a monument costing $1,500 was designed and built. It included a medallion of Poe by an artist named Valck. On 1 October 1875, his body was exhumed and re-interred close to the entrance to the church. At a dedication ceremony on 17 November, Neilson Poe described his cousin as 'one of the best-hearted men that ever lived'. The poet Walt Whitman was the only one of the poets invited who attended, although Alfred, Lord Tennyson contributed a poem that was read.

- The cause of Poe's death has been the subject of speculation for the more than 150 years since his death, mainly because his death certificate and medical reports have all been lost, if, indeed, they ever existed. There are countless theories as to what killed him, including a rare brain disease, a brain tumour, diabetes, enzyme deficiencies, syphilis, heart disease, epilepsy and meningeal inflammation. The newspapers of the day attributed it to 'congestion of the brain' or 'cerebral inflammation', both of which were simply euphemisms used at the time to disguise the disgrace of a death from alcoholism. In 2006, hairs from Poe's head were analysed and found not to contain heavy amounts of lead or mercury, thus discounting poisoning by those substances. Rabies was recently added to the list as well as cholera – he had been in Philadelphia in the winter of 1849 when a cholera epidemic had been raging. His friend Dr Snodgrass attributed his death to alcoholism and, being a passionate supporter of the temperance movement, used Poe as an example of the evil that can be done by the demon drink. This theory was refuted, however, in 1885, by Joseph Moran who said that Poe did not smell of alcohol when he brought him into the hospital. Others say that Poe was not a great drinker, unless under undue stress and one claimed that he would get drunk on just one glass of wine. When he died, he was a member of the Sons of Temperance.

- Poe's drug-taking is also disputed. A doctor friend said that if Poe had been an opium user, as has been claimed, he would have seen signs of it and he did not.

- One suggestion as to his cause of death is that he was a victim of the illegal practice of 'cooping' in which unwilling people were kidnapped and 'cooped' up in places where they were drugged or forced to drink whiskey until they did not know what they were doing. On election day, they were carried round and forced to vote in numerous wards. It was election day when Poe was found and he did repeat the name 'Reynolds'; one of the judges overseeing the Fourth Ward Polls at Ryan's Tavern was called Reynolds.

- Poe's image as a drug-addled drunk was created by one man – Rufus Wilmot Griswold, a well-known poet, editor and critic. He disliked Poe intensely and the character assassination he had carried out on him before his death was perpetuated after his death. Writing as 'Ludwig' he provided a bizarrely unpleasant obituary. He wrote of Poe walking the streets 'in madness or melancholy, with lips moving in indistinct curses' and described him as a 'brilliant, but erratic star'. Unfortunately, Poe's character, as described by Griswold, both in the obituary and in a biographical piece in a collection of Poe's work, became the accepted view of Poe. Readers became titillated by the thought of reading the work of a depraved character who resembled in many ways the characters he created.

- Many have tried to identify the owner of the name 'Reynolds' that Poe shouted out a number of times as he lay dying. Some have suggested Jeremiah N. Reynolds who was a newspaper editor and explorer and may have provided the inspiration for Poe's 1838 novel *The Narrative of Arthur Gordon Pym of Nantucket*. Others claim that it must have been Judge Henry R. Reynolds (see above).

- Edgar Allan Poe has been credited since his death with inventing detective fiction as well as science fiction. The annual awards given by the Mystery Writers of America are known as 'Edgars'.

- An essay written by Poe in 1848, *Eureka: a Prose Poem*, describes the Big Bang Theory, a full eighty years before it was scientifically proven. He also made influential contributions to cryptography and cosmology.

- Every year since 1949, a mystery visitor has toasted Poe's memory at his graveside. On 19 January, the man, known as the 'Poe Toaster', visits the grave in the early hours of the morning, toasts him with cognac and leaves three roses.

— ELVIS PRESLEY —

The Elvis Presley of 1977 was a very different person to the young lion who had exploded onto the music scene in Memphis more than twenty years previously, rewriting the rules of popular music and earning untold riches in the process. The Elvis of the late 1970s was a sad, bloated figure who had overindulged in pharmaceuticals and junk food for too long and whose stage performances were becoming increasingly shambolic and embarrassing.

On Monday 15 August 1977, he was preparing to leave his Memphis home, Graceland, for Portland, Maine where, two days later, he was due to launch a short tour. As usual, he woke at around four in the afternoon and three hours later, sent for his cousin Billy Smith.

In his daily life Elvis lived in a cocoon of sorts, surrounded by a coterie of friends and relatives who hovered around him like bees around a honey-pot. He expected these people to play according to his rules, however, and, as they fed off him, it could be said that, to a certain extent, he fed off them.

For years, Elvis would wake up, as on this day, in the late afternoon to begin his day. He would play racquetball, hire movie theatres and fun parks and live his life when the rest of the world was asleep. And he expected his friends to do the same – the women in his life and the so-called Memphis Mafia, consisting of boyhood friends and cousins who had been with him all the way on the fabulous ride that had been his career.

On this particular Monday, he wanted to arrange a screening of the film *Macarthur*, starring Gregory Peck. Ricky Stanley, Elvis' stepbrother – his father, Vernon had re-married after the death of Elvis' beloved mother, Gladys – was charged with organising the screening, but the cinema could not find a print of the film, so Elvis and Billy elected to just watch television.

Elvis had an appointment arranged with his dentist, Dr Hoffman, for 10.30 (even his physicians and dentists had to work on 'Elvis time') and asked Billy to call his girlfriend, Ginger Alden. He had first met twenty-year-old Ginger the previous November when she came out to visit at the house with her sister, Terry, the reigning Miss Tennessee. Everyone had thought Elvis would go for Terry, but it was only Ginger he had eyes for.

Dressed in a black Drug Enforcement Agency sweatsuit, with two forty-five revolvers stuffed in the waistband of his trousers, he left by the back stairs, accompanied by Ginger, Charlie and his cousin, Joe Esposito. Due to Elvis' swollen ankles, the zips on his black leather boots remained undone.

The dentist cleaned Elvis' teeth and filled a couple of small cavities and the party returned to Graceland soon after midnight in good spirits. Elvis' teeth felt fine, but he had made sure to get some codeine tablets just in case. He then went upstairs alone, calling down to Joe with some last-minute tour instructions and also making arrangements for his daughter, who had been visiting, to be flown back to California on a commercial flight.

Elvis and Ginger then picked up the threads of the argument they always had before a tour and once again she refused to fly out with him that night. But Elvis let it go and they talked, instead, about what would be the best date to get married.

Dr George Nichopoulos, known as Dr Nick, had been Elvis' personal physician for some years and he was not surprised to receive a call from the singer at 2.15 a.m. Elvis was having a little pain from one of the teeth that had been filled earlier and needed some painkillers. Ricky Stanley was sent out to the all-night pharmacy to pick up a prescription of six Dilaudid tablets.

All was quiet then until four in the morning when Billy and Joe received a call from Elvis asking if they wanted to play racquetball with him. On the way to the racquetball building it was raining and when Billy said he was sick of the rain, Elvis retorted: 'Ain't no problem. I'll take care of it.' He held up his hands and, coincidentally, the rain stopped.

They played a few games, but Elvis, unfit and carrying too much weight, tired rapidly and it quickly deteriorated into a game of dodgeball. When Elvis hit his shin with his racket they abandoned the game.

On the way out of the building Elvis sat down at a piano and sang. After a couple of familiar gospel standards, he launched into *Blue Eyes Crying in the Rain*, a song that had recently been a hit for Willie Nelson. It would be the last song Elvis sang.

Each night it took a large quantity of pills to get Elvis anywhere close to sleeping and, returning to his bedroom, he swallowed the first of three packets of pills containing Seconal, Placidyl, Valmid, Tuinol, Demerol and other depressants and placebos prescribed for him every night by Dr Nick. A few hours later, still unable to sleep, he took the second packet.

Elvis called down for the third packet a few hours later, but everyone had gone, including the nurse who stayed at the house on Dr Nick's behalf to dispense the singer's drugs. So, Elvis asked his Aunt Delta to call the nurse who got her husband to bring the packet to Graceland.

Elvis told his aunt that he would be getting up at around seven o'clock that evening and a short while later, still unable to sleep, he told Ginger that he was going to the bathroom to read.

At around 1.30 p.m. Ginger woke up and called her mother who asked how Elvis was. But she did not know, she told her, as he had not come back to bed. She washed, put make-up on and knocked on his bathroom door. There was no answer. She pushed the door open. Elvis lay on the floor, gold pyjama bottoms round his ankles, his face buried in a pool of vomit. She immediately called downstairs and asked for help.

Al Strada and Elvis' cousin Joe came running upstairs and Joe tried to revive him, but to no avail. The room quickly filled with people, including Elvis' father Vernon, who was distraught.

In the midst of this, Elvis' young daughter, Lisa arrived. 'What's wrong with my daddy?' she asked. But no one was in any doubt. The King of Rock and Roll's face was swollen and purple, his tongue was discoloured and sticking out of his mouth, his eyeballs were red.

Sometime on the morning of 16 August 1977, Elvis Presley had left the building.

 ## THE FUNERAL

Elvis was taken from the hospital to the Memphis Funeral Home where he was embalmed. He was buried on 17 August dressed in a white suit, white tie and a blue shirt. He had on a gold TCB (Taking Care of Business) lightning bolt ring and was in a 900-pound steel-lined copper coffin, flown in from Oklahoma.

The funeral service took place at the Wooddale Church of Christ with music provided by the old-fashioned quartet singers that Elvis grew up with. J. D. Sumner and the Stamps, The Statesmen, Jake Hess and James Blackwood all performed. Televangelist Rex Hubbard said a few words and Reverend C. W. Bradley presided.

A hundred vans carried the floral tributes to Forest Hill

Cemetery, taking nearly four hours. The copper coffin was borne in a white hearse, flanked by a police motorcycle escort. A silver Cadillac then led seventeen white limousines along roads lined with crowds of weeping people. Elvis's coffin was placed in a grey, marble-faced mausoleum a short distance from the grave of his mother.

☠ POST MORTEM

- Elvis' room was immediately cleaned up, the bed stripped and remade, the bathroom scrubbed. Not even the most common household remedies were to be found in the medicine cabinet. However, Shelby County Medical Investigator Dan Warlick reported seeing two empty syringes in the room.

- According to the autopsy, results of which were announced very soon – too soon, some would say – after Elvis' demise, 'death was due to cardiac arrhythmia due to undetermined heartbeat'. Two months later, the lab reports and analyses that were filed gave 'polypharmacy' as the more likely cause of death. The Biosciences report – giving the deceased's name as 'Ethel Moore' – listed fourteen drugs present in his system. There was ten times the safe level of Codeine, Quaalude in a toxic amount and other drugs at unsafe levels. The arguments about what actually killed Elvis rage on to this day.

- As news of Elvis' death began to spread, the local

telephone system collapsed under the weight of calls; the local florist received three thousand orders; and a crowd of fifty thousand people gathered on Elvis Presley Boulevard, outside Graceland.

- Thirty thousand people – including Caroline Kennedy and James Brown – shuffled into the vestibule of Graceland for the public viewing of the body. Police helicopters hovered over the mansion and the National Guard was called out to help the eighty policemen and forty sheriff's deputies trying to control the hysterical crowd.

- Elvis Presley's star is undiminished in death and in 2004, daughter Lisa Marie cut a deal with Robert FX Sillerman and his new media and entertainment company, CKX, Inc., to sell a majority interest in the assets comprising the estate of Elvis Presley. Sillerman paid about $100 million for eighty-five per cent of Lisa Marie Presley's interests in Elvis Presley Enterprises.

 THE CONSPIRACY THEORY

Rumours abound that Elvis is still alive, that he faked his death so that he could enjoy a normal life and there have been numerous sightings of him over the years. However, when a former employee of the Memphis Funeral Home was asked if he thought Elvis was really dead, he replied: 'Absolutely. I shoved the cotton balls up his ass when he was embalmed.'

— ABE 'KID TWIST' RELES —

His crumpled, broken body was found beneath the window of Room 623 of the Half Moon Hotel on Coney Island on 12 November 1941. Abe 'Kid Twist' Reles, Brooklyn's Public Enemy Number One and the most feared of all the hitmen employed by the Mafia's special killing machine, Lepke Buchalter's Murder Inc., would not be troubling anyone any more.

Reles had done the unthinkable. He had turned state's evidence and at the time of his death was only hours away from testifying against Murder Inc.'s chief executioner, Albert 'Mad Hatter' Anastasia and, in all likelihood, condemning him to die in the electric chair.

Reles, the son of Austrian Jewish immigrants, was born into poverty, like most Mafiosi and was said to have ice water running through his veins. A psychopath whose favourite method of despatch was an ice-pick inserted deep into the brain behind the ear, he thought nothing of employing extreme violence for the smallest of slights. He once killed a car-wash attendant who failed to remove a mark from the bumper of his car.

Kid Twist became one of Lepke's favourite killers. Murder Inc. had been assembled by the five Mafia crime families to take care of 'problems' and are thought to have been responsible for some eight hundred murders over the years. They were well rewarded – $12,000 a year, good money in the 1930s, plus pension and benefits. They also got to keep whatever they found on the bodies of their victims.

Things had started to go wrong in 1940 when the authorities enjoyed a lucky break. They picked up a small-time crook called Pretty Levine who told them about a killing that the Brooklyn crew had carried out. A man called Walter Sage had been skimming off the proceeds from the gang's slot machines. Sage was strangled, had an ice-pick stuck in his head – wielded, no doubt, by Kid Twist – and, in a neatly symbolic gesture, was tied to a pinball machine which was thrown into a lake in the Catskills.

Reles heard the cops were after him for the killing and turned himself in, certain that they had no real evidence, just like the half-dozen other times he had been brought in for questioning about a murder.

Not this time, however. A zealous district attorney, William O'Dwyer, was determined to put him away and they charged him with a number of murders. It seemed to the Kid that the game was up. He would be fingered for everything and would almost certainly end up in the electric chair. There was only one thing to do. He agreed to tell them all he knew.

For a year he was held in protective custody, at one point, when it was feared he was suffering from tuberculosis, in Harbour Hospital under the name of Albert Smith. Then, not long before the start of the trial, he was moved to the Half Moon Hotel, named after explorer Henry Hudson's ship that had anchored nearby in 1609 before setting sail to find a short-cut to Asia. Now and then, Reles and his fellow Murder Inc. stool pigeons Allie 'Tick Tock' Tannenbaum, Mickie Syckoff and Sholem Bernstein could be found exercising in a park on Long Island.

Reles sang for two weeks, providing gruesome details of eighty-five murders in Brooklyn. His information would later send Lepke himself to the chair and a number of his associates followed him, amongst whom were Harry 'Pittsburgh Phil' Strauss, Mendy Weiss, Harry 'Happy' Maione, Frank 'Dasher' Abbandando and Reles' loyal boyhood friend, Martin 'Bugsy' Goldstein.

On the morning of 13 November, however, the newspapers recorded not the end of the fearsome Anastasia, but the death of Kid Twist in a fatal fall from his hotel room window. 'The Canary Can Sing, But He Can't Fly' sneered the headlines.

 THE FUNERAL

Abe Reles was buried at Mount Carmel Cemetery in Queens, New York. The inscription on his tombstone reads 'Our Dear Brother'.

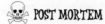 **POST MORTEM**

- A Grand Jury looking into Reles' death concluded that he 'met his death whilst trying to escape by means of a knotted sheet attached to a radiator in his room. We find that Reles did not meet with foul play and that he did die by suicide. It would be sheer speculation to attempt to disarm his motive for wanting to escape.'

- The case against Albert Anastasia collapsed and he went on to become the boss of the Mangano family, later to evolve into the Gambino family. He would die in 1957 in a hail of bullets in the barbershop of a New York hotel (see page 15).

 THE CONSPIRACY THEORY

- If it was an escape attempt, it was a pathetic one. The sheets found knotted to the radiator were a long way from the ground and safety. Trying to escape from five floors up did seem a little foolhardy.

- The body was found some twenty feet away from the wall of the hotel, suggesting that he was probably thrown.

- It was suggested that Frank Costello, head of the Luciano family, paid the five cops looking after Kid Twist to throw him from the window. It seems likely the police guard was involved. The area that Reles and his fellow state's witnesses were being held had been sealed off with a steel door and was said to be impregnable. The statements given by the officers on duty were inconsistent and they could not agree on many basic things.

- Some hinted that everyone was involved – the cops, the district attorney and the Mob.
- One theory had it that the Kid was pretending to escape but his practical joke went wrong.
- William O'Dwyer became mayor of New York, but when it looked certain he would be indicted for corruption, he fled to Mexico.

FRANKLIN DELANO ROOSEVELT

He had been president since 1932 and when he was re-elected in 1944, it seemed unlikely that Franklin Delano Roosevelt would make it to the end of his unprecedented fourth term in office. By March 1945, he was beginning to pay the price of steering his country through two of its greatest crises – the Depression and World War Two.

He had suffered from poor health for many years. In 1921 he had been stricken with poliomyelitis, a viral infection of the nerve fibres of the spinal cord, probably contracted while swimming in stagnant lake water while on holiday. He was, from then on, effectively paralysed from the waist down and used leg braces to walk, or give the impression that he was walking.

On the afternoon of 30 March, he arrived at what was known as the Little White House in Warm Springs, Georgia, for a short break. The Georgia air suited the president and his health usually improved when he was there. This visit was no different and he soon settled into a balanced routine of work and pleasure.

On Monday 9 April, Lucy Rutherfurd, accompanied by her painter friend Elizabeth Shoumatoff, arrived to spend the final week of the vacation with the president. He had met Lucy when he was Assistant Secretary of the Navy, and he became quite taken with her. Shoumatoff was to paint a portrait of the president during their stay.

On 11 April, Roosevelt worked on a draft of his upcoming Jefferson Day speech and around noon the following day, Shoumatoff began work on the portrait. The president sat for her in the living room of the house dressed in a double-breasted grey suit and wearing a crimson tie. Surrounded by Lucy and several others, he worked his way through a stack of papers as Shoumatoff sketched.

At around 1 p.m., Roosevelt's butler served lunch. The president suddenly seemed agitated and appeared to flinch visibly in his chair. An assistant asked him if he needed help. Suddenly, his head fell forward. Gripping it with his left hand, he whispered, 'I have a terrific headache.' They were the last words he would utter. He collapsed and lost consciousness.

He was immediately taken to his bedroom and his physician Dr Bruenn, who had accompanied him to Warm Springs, was summoned. By this time, Roosevelt's breathing had stopped, desperate attempts were made at artificial respiration and he was given an injection of adrenaline into his heart.

At 3.35 p.m., Franklin Delano Roosevelt, thirty-second President of the United States, was pronounced dead of a massive cerebral haemorrhage, aged sixty-three.

 # THE FUNERAL

Roosevelt's declining health was unknown to the public at large and his death caused an outbreak of shocked grief in the United States and around the world.

His body was taken by train 1,100 miles from Warm Springs to Washington D.C. and then on to the Roosevelt family estate in New York. His tomb lists only his name and dates of birth and death. Fala, his beloved Scottish terrier, is buried a few yards from him.

 ## POST MORTEM

- Vice President Harry Truman arrived at the White House at 5.30 p.m. Within ninety minutes, the Cabinet had been assembled, and Truman had been sworn in as the thirty-third President of the United States.
- Newsflashes on the radio brought the nation the first news of Roosevelt's death. Listeners to Tom Mix on the Mutual Broadcasting System and children listening to the Daniel Boone serial *Wilderness Road* on CBS were shocked by broadcast interruptions announcing the death.
- The *New York Times* editorial statement read: 'Men will thank God on their knees, a hundred years from now, that Franklin Delano Roosevelt was in the White House ... in that dark hour when a powerful and ruthless barbarism threatened to overrun civilization.'

- Winston Churchill did not attend Roosevelt's funeral and it is claimed that, for that reason, many years later, President Lyndon Johnson did not attend Churchill's funeral.
- Within a month of Roosevelt's death, the Allies were claiming victory in Europe.
- Elizabeth Shoumatoff's portrait was never finished and is known, unsurprisingly, as *The Unfinished Portrait*.
- On 3 January 2000, Roosevelt was named first runner-up (behind Albert Einstein) as *Time* magazine's Man of the Century.

— ALAN SEEGER —

'We go up to the attack tomorrow. This will probably be the biggest thing yet. We are to have the honour of marching in the first wave. I will write you soon if I get through all right. If not, my only earthly care is for my poems. I am glad to be going in the first wave. If you are in this thing at all it is best to be in to the limit. And this is the supreme experience.'

American poet Alan Seeger, who wrote the lines above to a friend, had graduated from Harvard in 1910, moving to Paris' bohemian Left Bank after spending two years in Greenwich Village in New York. At the outbreak of war he had joined the French Foreign Legion, in order to help defend his beloved France.

Thus, on the morning of 4 July 1916, he found himself at the front, eager to throw himself into the killing machine that was World War One. However, his company was disappointed to be given the news, at around nine o'clock that morning, that they were to be held in reserve. Instead of going over the top, they were to spend the morning unloading eight-inch shells from the trucks that had brought them up to the front.

As time passed, things seemed to be going well. Thousands of prisoners were being brought in and the colonial regiments appeared to be making progress. More ominously, however, a continuous stream of ambulances snaked along the roads leading away from the battlefield. As Seeger and his comrades left their work to talk to those who had been close to the action, the order suddenly rang out to fall in.

At around four o'clock the command finally came to prepare for the assault. Two battalions were to attack the village of Belloy-en-Santerre, and Seeger's company was to form the reserve of battalion. The companies forming the first wave readied themselves on the plain, bayonets glinting in the sunlight.

Seeger's section formed the right and vanguard of the company. On the command, all rushed forward and then threw themselves to the ground. A friend of the poet, in another section, watched as Seeger's section swung round to the right of Belloy-en-Santerre. He caught sight of the poet and called to him, waving his hand in his direction. The friend wrote later that Seeger answered his call with a smile. He stood out, being the tallest man in the section.

Running forward with his bayonet fixed, he disappeared into the village and was never seen again.

☠ POST MORTEM

- The price of sixty thousand casualties that day did not seem too high for Allied military command. They ordered the offensive to continue next day. Eventually after a bloody summer and autumn, a million men had perished — 420,000 British, 200,000 French and 500,000 Germans.

- The result of the offensive was a gain of all of six miles.
- Alan Seeger was the uncle of the famous American folk singer, Pete Seeger.

— AYRTON SENNA —

THURSDAY 28 APRIL 1994

Ayrton Senna, the greatest racing driver of his or, perhaps, any generation, arrived at the Imola circuit for the San Marino Grand Prix by helicopter, accompanied by the president of Ducati, the motorcycle manufacturer which was producing a Senna motorbike, and the CEO of TAG-Heuer, who were working on a Senna watch. Senna visited his team, Williams, before heading off to his hotel.

He had moved to the all-conquering Williams that season from the familiar McLaren team with whom he had won three world championships. Expected to start winning immediately, two races into the new season they had not won a single point. Adding to his anguish at this lack of success was his suspicion that the Ferrari of his great rival, Michael Schumacher, which had taken the honours in those first two races, was illegal.

He arrived at his hotel at around five. The Castello, just outside Castel San Pietro, ten kilometres west of Imola, was traditionally the McLaren team hotel but Senna had stayed there for the San Marino Grand Prix every year since 1989, always booking the same room and he was not about to change because of the move to Williams.

That first evening, Senna ate steak, pasta and his favourite profiteroles, before retiring at around ten o'clock. The Castello always made sure there was a large supply of profiteroles when he was in residence.

FRIDAY 29 APRIL

Friday was taken up with free practice during which Senna completed twenty-two laps, recording a time more than a second faster than his team-mate Damon Hill. But as he was returning to the pits, the Jordan of fellow Brazilian Rubens Barrichello had a horrific crash.

Ayrton Senna took a great interest in driver safety, to the extent of having outlined plans for an independent commission to oversee safety matters. He went immediately to the medical centre to check on Barrichello's condition, vaulting a fence at the back on finding the front door locked. The first face Barrichello saw on regaining consciousness after the accident was his compatriot. 'He had tears in his eyes,' Barrichello recalls. 'I had never seen that with Ayrton before. I just had the impression he felt as if my accident was like one of his own.'

Soon, however, Senna was back racing. He immediately bettered his time and then recorded the best time of the entire weekend, a characteristically brilliant achievement, given his emotional state after Barrichello's crash, coupled with his lack of familiarity with the Williams.

But still, he was not satisfied with the car. He talked for a while to his race engineer, David Brown, and later cut short a press interview because of the problems with the Williams. One of the journalists claims that Senna was not his usual focused self: 'His answers were halting and he looked glazed as if he was mentally worn out.'

He left the circuit at eight and dined in a small restaurant in Castel San Pietro. He ate the meal he always ate there – antipasti, Parma ham, tagliatelle with a plain tomato sauce and fruit. No coffee, no alcohol and his mineral water carbonated and slightly warm. And, for once, no profiteroles. At eleven he returned to his room.

SATURDAY 30 APRIL

On Saturday morning Senna completed nineteen laps in the second free practice session. At one o'clock, however, the second qualifying session began with a disaster. The Simtek of Roland Ratzenberger, the popular Austrian driver, hit a concrete wall on the Villeneuve curve at almost 200 mph. Ratzenberger was seriously injured, being rushed immediately to the medical centre and then airlifted to a hospital in Bologna where he was tragically pronounced dead, Formula One's first fatality since 1982.

Senna had watched the accident on a monitor as it happened and is said to have gone to the back of the garage, covering his face with his hands. He then left the Williams garage, commandeered a safety car and drove to the scene of the accident, arriving just after Ratzenberger had been taken away, but seeing the carnage left behind.

Returning to the pits, he was told of Ratzenberger's death by Professor Sid Watkins, the head of the FIA medical commission. Watkins says Senna was 'very shocked. He had never faced the reality of his profession before so starkly because no one had been killed during his time in Formula One. He was always fatalistic about death; he was a religious man and intelligent enough to think it through.'

Martin Whitaker, FIA press officer, asked Senna what had happened and Senna did not reply. 'He just looked at me and walked away,' Whitaker says. 'I won't forget the look. To say it was fear would be over the top. He was just very worried. There was something different about him. You can see it in the photos of him that weekend.'

Williams withdrew from further racing that day and Senna returned to his motorhome where he was alone with Damon Hill and his wife who tried to calm him. His spirits were very low and he declined to attend the traditional pole winner's press conference. The FIA decided not to fine him for this breach of the regulations.

Around three in the afternoon, the stewards did summon Senna, however, to reprimand him for his use of the safety car.

But he was in no mood to accept their censure. There was a heated exchange, Senna claiming that he, a three-times world champion, represented all the drivers and that he seemed to be the only one concerned about safety.

Following this, he returned to his hotel, reportedly looking dreadful. He called his girlfriend, Adriane Galisteu, twice that evening. In the first call, shortly before dinner, he told her he did not feel like racing the next day, that he felt it would be morally wrong to race. 'He was shaken,' she says. 'Crying, really crying. He told me he did not want to race. He had never spoken like that.' When she suggested that he did not have to race, he thought about it and replied that it was his job; he had to.

After a sombre dinner, he went to see Frank Williams, head of the team. By this time he was calmer and confirmed to Williams his readiness to drive the next day. When he called Adriane again, he seemed to be in a much better frame of mind. He told her to come and pick him up at Faro airport the following night and that he could not wait to see her.

They were the last words he would speak to her.

SUNDAY 1 MAY

On Sunday, race day, Senna flew to the track and was again fastest in the morning warm-up. He instructed David Brown not to change anything on the car and then did a televised lap for the French station TF1, for whom his old rival Alain Prost was working. Somewhat unexpectedly, given the bitter enmity between the two and the fact that they had not spoken for years, Senna called in over the radio, 'I would like to say welcome to my old friend, Alain Prost. Tell him we miss him very much.' Prost was touched and the pair later talked for some time in the paddock. Senna wanted Prost to be involved in his safety commission and they agreed to meet before the Monaco Grand Prix two weeks later. That morning, he also recruited former world champion Nicky Lauda to his cause.

At the eleven o'clock drivers' briefing, the drivers held a minute's silence for Ratzenberger and an animated discussion ensued, Senna criticising the use of the pace car on the warm-up lap, claiming it did not allow the cars' tyres to warm up sufficiently. He was also concerned about the safety car's speed. Afterwards he went reluctantly to the Williams hospitality area where he and Damon Hill entertained Williams' sponsors and guests.

At midday, he began his preparations for the race, eating a light lunch and then shutting himself away. Before a race, he would often read the Bible he carried in his briefcase.

Thirty minutes before the start he went to the pits where a Brazilian journalist asked him to sign three pictures. In the pictures, Senna looked uncharacteristically gaunt and pale and they were to shock and haunt the Brazilian nation for weeks after his death. The journalist claims that Senna did something he never did: 'He walked round the car, looked at the tyres, rested on the rear wing, almost as if he was suspicious of the car.'

At two o'clock, led by Senna in pole position, the cars set out on their warm-up lap, but there were problems immediately when Pedro Lamy's Lotus rear-ended J. J. Lehto's Benetton which had stalled on the line. There was debris everywhere and, adding to the air of misfortune already hanging over the weekend, a wheel spun off over the safety fencing into the crowd, injuring nine people. The safety car was deployed and Senna followed it, Michael Schumacher, Gerhard Berger and Damon Hill behind him. When the Williams team radioed that the safety car was about to pull off, Senna acknowledged the message. It would be his last contact.

The race began in earnest, and he and Schumacher immediately opened up a gap on the rest of the field.

Seventeen minutes into the race, taking the fast Tamburello curve for the second time, Senna's Williams veered inexplicably off the track at 190 mph, slamming into an unprotected concrete retaining wall. The front right side of the car took most of the impact, a wheel was ripped off and the vehicle bounced back off the wall onto the track. In the split second before it hit the wall, Senna had managed to slow the Williams to 130 mph. That, plus the fact that the monocoque had remained intact and that a slight movement of his head was visible, gave cause for hope. Tragically, however, he had suffered massive head injuries and unfortunate aerial pictures of the car, surrounded with Senna's blood, were transmitted into millions of homes.

He was lifted from the wreckage and airlifted by helicopter to the same Bologna hospital to which Ratzenberger had been taken, doctors on board fighting to save him.

Meanwhile, thirty-seven minutes later, the race was re-started. Senna's friend Berger led for the first eleven laps but retired on lap fourteen, going straight from the circuit to the hospital.

Meanwhile, Adriane Galisteu had been watching on television. She was telephoned to say that a plane had been arranged for her to fly to Senna's bedside. It was turned back not long after take-off.

The race was won by Michael Schumacher but no one really cared. Shortly after the end of the race, at around 4.20, tests confirmed that Senna was brain-dead and was being kept alive only by artificial means.

At 6.40 p.m. Ayrton Senna da Silva was pronounced dead.

 ## THE FUNERAL

Senna was given a state funeral in Brazil and was buried at the Morumbi Cemetery near São Paulo, a cemetery dedicated to Brazil's finest. More than fifty thousand people watched his funeral cortege.

Given their bitter rivalry, Alain Prost was worried about the reception he would receive if he attended the funeral. However, he was persuaded to go and his gesture was appreciated by Senna's fans.

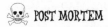

POST MORTEM

- In the shattered remains of Senna's car, they discovered a furled Austrian flag. Senna had intended to dedicate his forty-second grand prix victory to Roland Ratzenberger's memory.

- Michael Schumacher blamed himself for Senna's accident and is reported to have been distraught in his motorhome after the race. He said it was his fault because he pushed Senna too hard. He did not attend the funeral.

- In 2001, a Channel 4 television documentary suggested that the crash might have been the result of an unusually long safety-car period that had reduced the pressures in Senna's tyres, thereby lowering the car. Therefore, it claimed, as the car entered the Tamburello bend, it bottomed out and the loss of the ground effect led to a sudden reduction in downforce and, hence, grip. As Senna instinctively corrected the resultant slide, the downforce and grip suddenly returned, and Senna effectively drove off the circuit. The programme came to the ironic conclusion that if Senna hadn't been such a great driver, his reactions to the slide wouldn't have been as quick, and he might have survived the crash.

- Senna did not like the position of the steering column relative to his seating position and had repeatedly asked for it to be changed. Patrick Head and Adrian Newey agreed to modify the steering column and many surmise, based on video evidence of Senna turning the wheel left and right with no movement of the front wheels, that steering failure was the cause of the crash.

- The Williams designers Patrick Head and Adrian Newey were charged with manslaughter as a result of the accident, which the Italian prosecution argued was caused by the failure of an improperly welded steering column on Senna's car. They were acquitted in 1997 but the prosecution appealed the verdict. It took two more years before the appeal court rejected prosecution demands for one-year suspended sentences against Head, the technical director of the Williams team, and Newey, formerly the team's chief designer who took over as technical director at the rival McLaren team in 1997. The case was surprisingly reopened in 2004.

- Senna's wrecked Williams, and his damaged racing helmet, were destroyed following the 1999 acquittal.

— TUPAC SHAKUR —

In September 1996, rap artist Tupac Shakur was persuaded to go to Las Vegas by Marion 'Suge' Knight, CEO of the infamous rap record label Deathrow Records. Tupac told his girlfriend, Kidada, that he had promised Suge that he would accompany him to a heavyweight boxing match featuring Mike Tyson at the MGM Grand in Vegas and that he could not let him down.

At his house in Calabasas, they prepared to leave, Kidada packing their suitcases. When she reached for the bulletproof vest that Tupac always wore, he told her not to bring it, 'It would be too hot,' he said.

Travelling to Vegas by car, they stopped at a petrol station where Tupac bought five magazines, all of them about guns. He read these all the way to their hotel, the Luxor, from where they drove to Suge's mansion, where Tupac videoed the record executive making some phone calls.

The fight that night was between Mike Tyson and Bruce Seldon and Suge annoyed Tupac by turning up at the last minute. Nonetheless, he was excited by the fight. 'Did you see Tyson do it to him?' he said excitedly. 'Tyson did it to him!

Did ya'll see that? We bad like that. Come out of prison and now we running shit.' He went backstage and congratulated Tyson.

8.45 p.m.: Tupac got into a fight with a man called Orlando Anderson, a member of a rival gang who had recently created trouble for a Deathrow employee. The Deathrow crew joined in and Anderson was beaten to a pulp. The fight, recorded by a CCTV camera, was stopped by hotel security and the victim of the beating, after being held for questioning by the police, was allowed to leave, declining to press charges.

8.55 p.m.: Tupac went back to his hotel at around this time. He saw a car belonging to the rap star MC Hammer and went over to tell him about the incident. He boasted that it took Mike Tyson fifty punches to beat Selden, but he put his man down with only three punches. At the hotel he told Kidada: 'Some nigga started a fight with me for nothin ... Something's up, you stay here.' He changed clothes and returned to Suge's house. He was due to perform at a party at Club 662 and had wanted to drive his Hummer, but Suge said that they had things to discuss and persuaded Tupac to ride with him.

10.50 p.m.: They left Suge's mansion in the label owner's black BMW 750 with tinted windows. Tupac was in the passenger seat, and a ten-car entourage followed them. Playing very low on the sound system was Tupac's new album, *The Don Killuminati: The 7 Day Theory*.

10.55 p.m.: Tupac rolled down the car window and a photographer took their picture at a red light.

11 p.m.: They were stopped on Las Vegas Boulevard by Metro bicycle cops for playing the car stereo too loud and for not having licence plates. These were in the trunk of the car.

11.15 p.m.: At a red light on Flamingo Road, near the intersection of Koval Lane, in front of the Maxim Hotel, two girls distracted Tupac and Suge on the driver's side, and a white, four-door, late-model Cadillac with California plates pulled up. Tupac had been standing up, the upper part of his body through the sunroof. Two of the four men inside the other car got out and fired thirteen rounds into the passenger side of the car, from a Glock .40 calibre handgun. Tupac desperately tried to get into the backseat, but Suge pulled him down and a bullet bounced off his right hip bone and hit his lung. He was also hit in his right hand and chest. Suge was hit too, but suffered only a minor head wound.

Immediately after the shooting, the Cadillac headed south on Koval. Suge made a U-turn from the left lane of Flamingo and sped west towards Las Vegas Boulevard, *away* from the nearest hospital. Suge said that he told Tupac he'd get him to a hospital, and Tupac replied: 'I need a hospital? You're the one shot in the head.'

Patrol officers on an unrelated call at the Maxim Hotel had heard the gunshots and called for backup. Two other officers followed the BMW, which took a left on Las Vegas Boulevard South. Police reached the car when it was caught in traffic at the intersection of Las Vegas Boulevard and Harmon Avenue. They called an ambulance immediately. Inside, the BMW was splattered with blood and pieces of gold from Tupac's jewellery. The car had two flat tyres.

They took Tupac out of the car and placed him on a stretcher. He was complaining that he couldn't breathe. The ambulance then took the two men to the University of Nevada Medical Centre. When the police questioned the bodyguard they continuously asked if he had shot back, but he told them he had left his gun in the other car. The bodyguard thought it was Suge's friends who had shot back at the assailants. Yafeu Fula of Tupac's backing group the Outlaws Immortalz – fatally shot at a later date – had been in the car behind the BMW with bodyguards. He told the police that he could do a photo line-up, but there were suspicions immediately that the man they had beaten earlier, Orlando Anderson, was behind the shooting.

Tupac lost a great deal of blood on the way to the hospital and as he was being carried to the emergency room he moaned, 'I'm dying'. He had been admitted in a critical condition with injuries including a gunshot wound to his right chest with a massive hemothorax and a gunshot wound to the right thigh. A bullet had also fractured a finger on his right hand.

Just before midnight, he was taken to the hospital's Trauma Centre. He was resuscitated in the recovery area and was then put on life-support machines. Two litres of blood that had haemorrhaged into his chest cavity were removed. He was then taken to the operating room where he underwent emergency surgery. The procedure finished at 2.35 a.m.

Another operation began at 6.25 p.m. to remove his punctured right lung in order to stop the internal bleeding. He was back in his room at 7.45 and was put in a medicinally induced coma and on life support to take the pressure off his body.

Meanwhile, three sections of the LA gang the Bloods met at Lueders Park and talked about retaliation against their mortal enemies, the Southside Crips, for the attack on Tupac who was himself a Blood. At 2.58 p.m., on 9 August, a man who Las Vegas police said may have been in the Cadillac was shot in the back on East Alondra.

Tupac opened his eyes once, while Kidada was putting Don McLean's *Vincent* into a cassette player next to his bed. She asked him if he could hear her and told him to move his feet if he did. He moved them. She then asked if he knew she loved him. He nodded before sinking into a coma.

On the eleventh, Bobby Finch, a Southside Crip who Compton police officers said may have also been in the Cadillac, was gunned down on South Mayo. Suge and three lawyers spoke with Metro police for an hour but were not much help.

On 12 September, Tupac had been due to go to court for sentencing after his conviction for carrying a concealed gun. Instead, he was fighting for his life.

Next day, doctors tried to resuscitate him several times before his mother, the former Black Panther Afeni Shakur, asked them not to try again.

At 4.03 p.m. on Friday 13 September, Tupac Shakur was pronounced dead of respiratory failure and cardiopulmonary arrest.

THE FUNERAL

Tupac was cremated and his mother, Afeni, spread some of his ashes on a hill in LA and some on her garden.

A private funeral was held for him in Las Vegas and on 15 September there was a memorial service for him at The House of the Lord Pentecostal Church in Brooklyn, where he was still listed as a member of the congregation.

POST MORTEM

- As Tupac lay dying, Suge ranted at the bodyguard who had forgotten his gun. His threats were interrupted by a phone call informing him that Tupac was dead. Suge then told the bodyguard that it didn't matter now because he was gone, and, according to the bodyguard 'his voice was cracking up like he was going to cry'.

- An autopsy determined that Tupac didn't have any illegal drugs in his body, but he had been heavily sedated.

- Two detectives took Polaroid pictures of Tupac at the morgue for a police training book, but these were later removed from the book and destroyed.

- Two more Bloods gang members were shot and killed by an assailant who fled on foot.
- Police had thought that Orlando Anderson might have been a suspect, but he was ruled out because he was still being held when Tupac had left the building.
- Because Tupac didn't have a will, Afeni had to file court papers as his only living heir. Deathrow emptied his apartment, taking all the furniture.
- In December 1996, Tupac's new album went platinum.
- Orlando Anderson was shot dead in Compton in 1999 following a gun battle that left two other men dead.
- On the tenth anniversary of Tupac's death, Afeni Shakur met Nelson Mandela and spread the remainder of her son's ashes in South Africa.

 ### THE CONSPIRACY THEORY

Rumours persist amongst fans that Tupac did not actually die. They are suspicious for a number of reasons:

1. No pictures were ever released of Tupac in hospital.
2. Tupac raps about his own funeral on the track *Life Goes On*.
3. The video for the track *Mad at Cha*, released a few days after his death, shows Tupac as an angel and, in the video, Tupac was shot after leaving a theatre with a friend, which is not too dissimilar to how he was shot in real life.

4. In the video for *Hail Mary*, released under the name Makaveli, there is a gravestone that says Makaveli. But the gravestone is cracked and there is a hole right in front of it, inferring that Makaveli rose from the dead.

5. Tupac always wore a bulletproof vest, no matter where he went. Why did he not wear it at a very public event like the Tyson fight?

6. In a number of his songs he talks about being buried, so why was he cremated?

7. Tupac's alias was Makaveli. Machiavelli, the sixteenth-century Italian philosopher, advocated the staging of one's death in order to evade one's enemies and gain power. Tupac studied Machiavelli in depth while in prison. The title of the new album by Makaveli (Tupac) was *The 7 Day Theory*. Tupac was shot on 7 September and survived on the 7th, 8th, 9th, 10th, 11th, 12th, 'dying' on the 13th. Hence the title *The 7 Day Theory*.

- Further rumours claim that Tupac was not killed by Orlando Anderson, but that the killing was set up by Suge Knight who was angry that the rapper was going to leave Deathrow Records.

— DYLAN THOMAS —

Where Dylan Thomas is concerned, the glass is, for some, always half-empty – in their opinion, he squandered his talent in a sea of alcohol. For others, the man is indivisible from the life and in their minds, Dylan is forever holding a pen in one hand and a glass of whisky in the other. For Dylan, of course, the glass was always full … then empty … then full … then …

It was October 1953, and he had not wanted to return to New York so soon. Nonetheless, having already visited in the spring of that year, he found himself there again to take part in a performance of his 'play for voices', *Under Milk Wood*, at the Kaufmann Auditorium.

It had been a morose poet who had left London – he gave the thumbs-down sign to his friend Harry Locke, as his coach departed Victoria Air Terminal and his mood was not improved by a drunken Irish priest who had to be locked in one of the toilets and was then removed from the plane at a fuel stop in Newfoundland. The fact that by this time Dylan was referring to his wife, Caitlin, as 'my widow' did not bode well for the trip.

He had been ailing for some time, mainly as a result of his excessive drinking and one night, as they rehearsed the play, he was again taken ill. His American mistress, Liz Reitell, had brought a friend, Herbert Hannum, along that evening and as he sat with the poet whose temperature was fluctuating wildly, Hannum covered him with overcoats and provided him with hot-water bottles. At one point, Dylan threw up on the green-room floor and, as Hannum tried to move him to a couch, the poet grabbed him by the lapels and whispered: 'I've seen the gates of hell tonight.' Next day, Liz Reitell and Hannum persuaded him to see the doctor who had treated him during his last visit in the spring, Dr Milton Feltenstein.

It was Dylan's thirty-ninth birthday on 27 October, an ominous anniversary. He had said ever since he was a boy that he would not live to see forty. However, around this time, the poet W. H. Auden spotted him going into the Chelsea Hotel, Dylan's customary residence in New York, and reported that, contrary to reports, he looked neither drunk nor on the verge of death.

But Dylan was still living dangerously, and he was seen to take Benzedrine while drinking with a rowdy group of friends. He was also reported to have pushed a woman out of his cab in the early hours of the morning on his way back to his hotel.

It was 3 November, election day, and Dylan expressed his cynicism about politics to a stream of visitors he received in his room. That afternoon he was due to have a meeting with an agent about lecture tours and Liz asked everyone to leave so that she could get Dylan to stop drinking and make him and the room presentable. The meeting was successful, the agent guaranteeing him an income of at least $1,000 while on tour, a decent sum of money back then and Thomas' biggest break in years.

But, the meeting over, the poet became depressed and lay down on his bed. He started to reminisce to Liz about his home town, Laugharne, and then announced without warning that he wanted to die. Liz tried to console him, but he began to weep uncontrollably. Eventually, though, he fell asleep, not waking until two in the morning. He then insisted that he had to go out for a drink and to get some air. Liz, exhausted, no longer had the energy to try to stop him.

An hour-and-a-half later, he arrived back, drunk and swaying: 'I've had about eighteen straight whiskies. I think that's a record.' Of course, Dylan was known to exaggerate his drinking, but eighteen whiskies or not, it was obvious that, yet again, he had drunk to excess.

He then proceeded to fall asleep, his head in her lap.

When he awoke, he said he could not breathe and insisted on going out. Liz went with him this time, to the White Horse Tavern where, after only a couple of beers, he announced that he was unwell. Back at the hotel she called Dr Feltenstein who paid the first of the day's three visits to the hotel. He administered a steroid, ACTH, but the poet was still in pain from gastritis and gout.

By the third visit, it was evident from the fact that Dylan was experiencing mild hallucinations, that the medication was not working and Liz was convinced he was in the grip of delirium tremens. To calm him, the doctor administered a sedative.

Hospital records show that, given his breathing difficulties, he was given an unusually high, and potentially lethal, dose of morphine sulphate. The doctor has always refused to confirm or deny what he actually gave Dylan that night.

Exhausted, Liz had by now asked the painter Jack Heliker to come and help her look after Dylan. But shortly after he arrived, the poet began to rave alarmingly about the terrible things tormenting his mind. These were now geometric shapes, he claimed. Heliker kept watch as Liz lay down beside Dylan and tried to sleep.

Heliker says that Dylan woke up around midnight, saying, 'After thirty-nine years, this is all I've done.' Liz, however, maintains that his last words actually were 'Yes, I believe you,' in response to her telling him that the horrors rampaging through his mind would disappear.

Suddenly, she felt his grip tighten on her hand and Heliker records that his face started to turn blue. Within minutes, the poet was in an ambulance speeding towards the Roman Catholic hospital, St Vincent's. Perhaps, some have said since, Dr Feltenstein should have sent him there several hours previously.

He was admitted at 1.58 a.m., the medical notes stating that he arrived in a coma and that 'the impression upon admission was acute alcoholic encephalopathy damage to the brain by alcohol, for which the patient was treated without response'.

John Malcolm Brinnin, who had organised Dylan's visit to the States was called in Cambridge by a hysterical Liz Reitell and arrived at St Vincent's at seven in the morning of 4 November. Dylan, still in a coma, was receiving oxygen and blood transfusions and was diagnosed variously as suffering from liver failure, diabetes and a vague condition described as 'gross insult to the brain'. He did not seem to be in danger of death, but his comatose state gave rise to concerns about brain damage when, and if, he came round.

Brinnin called agent David Higham in London and asked him to tell Caitlin. Ironically, when the message arrived, she was in the midst of a group of friends and neighbours listening to a radio broadcast Dylan had made about Laugharne.

Caitlin finally made it to New York on the morning of Sunday 8 November. She was spared immigration at Idlewild Airport, thanks to a considerate British Embassy, and given a motorcycle escort to St Vincent's where, on seeing Brinnin, the first thing she is reported to have said was, 'Well, is the bloody man still alive?' By this time, a tracheotomy had been performed on the writer, who remained in his coma, and rumours and accusations were flying among the assembled friends and acquaintances.

Caitlin became very agitated on seeing Dylan, emerging from his room after only fifteen minutes and banging her head hard on a window. She was taken home by friends of the poet to rest.

Returning that afternoon, she almost pulled Dylan's tubes out as she tried to embrace him and worried the nursing staff by smoking dangerously close to the oxygen tent that surrounded him. She was given whiskey to calm her, but became violent instead, attacking Brinnin and the hospital staff who were trying to restrain her. She was put in a straitjacket and removed from the hospital to a mental institution for her own safety.

The following day, the poet's condition worsened. Fans, most of whom were unknown to Brinnin, filled the hospital waiting room. When he stepped out into the hospital corridor to get some air, he saw the American poet John Berryman rushing towards him. 'He's dead! He's dead!' he shouted. 'Where were you?'

Dylan died leaving little money and with no will.

POST MORTEM

- The post mortem gave the primary cause of death as pneumonia, with pressure on the brain and a fatty liver given as contributing factors.
- A memorial service took place at St Luke's Episcopal Church of Trinity Parish, New York, on Friday 13 November. Over four hundred people attended.
- That afternoon the body was put on the liner SS *United States*. Friends armed with champagne remained with Caitlin in her cabin until the ship left. By this time, she said, she was 'mad, drunk and heartbroken'. She ordered five double whiskies in the ship's bar and sat down and drank them slowly. She then leapt up and executed what she later

described as a 'mad dance of destruction', sweeping glasses off tables and doing high kicks, splits and cartwheels amongst the debris. The captain got some seamen to take her down to a bunk in the hold where she found some of the sailors were playing cards on Dylan's coffin. 'Dylan would have liked that,' she thought.

- At Southampton docks, a friend, Billy Williams, was waiting with a vehicle to transport Caitlin and the coffin back to Laugharne. On the way, they stopped at several pubs and then some hours later, found themselves in Devon, having taken a wrong turning.

 THE FUNERAL

The funeral took place at St Martin's Church, Laugharne. Caitlin is reported to have been howling like a wolf. At Brown's Hotel she knocked a tray of drinks out of Fred Janes' hands and he was soaked in beer from head to foot. When someone offered her a box of chocolates she threw them at the ceiling in a rage. Fights broke out in different parts of town, and someone tried to break into Dylan's workshed, looking for souvenirs. One woman was reported to be wandering around the town offering herself to any man who would have her.

― HUNTER S. THOMPSON ―

In his final years, Hunter S. Thompson had retreated to what he always termed a 'fortified compound' near Aspen in Colorado. His Woody Creek hideout became a destination for actors such as Johnny Depp, Benicio del Toro and Sean Penn, but Thompson was generally thought to have lost his literary momentum in recent times. Two plastic hips and illness had not helped, even though his weekly column for the website of the American sports network ESPN enjoyed some moments that recalled the highpoints of his Gonzo style of the 1960s and 1970s.

Hunter was reported to be in despair over the November 2004 re-election of George W. Bush. 'There has to be some defence against having this government in vain, seize, take over, invade our lives and our personal privacy every day,' he complained in an interview early in 2005.

In spite of all this, Hunter had been in fairly good spirits. As ever, he was living at a different time to everyone else, waking up late afternoon and beginning the regime of drugs and drink that had fortified him for many years. Now and then he would grab one of his beloved guns and go out and shoot something.

Several years before his demise, he had mistakenly shot and wounded his assistant.

He would write and make calls and send faxes to his friends. Occasionally, in the middle of the night, he would call his old partner in crime, the illustrator Ralph Steadman, at his home in Kent – his 'castle', as Hunter called it – and talk about recreating the magic of *Fear and Loathing in Las Vegas* one last time.

It was a Sunday and his son, Juan, was visiting. Hunter had gone into the next room to telephone his wife, Anita. She says her husband had asked her to come home from the health club she was visiting so they could work on his ESPN column. 'I was on the phone with him,' she reported. 'He set the receiver down and he did it. I heard the clicking of the gun.' She then said she heard a loud, muffled noise, but did not know what had happened. 'I was waiting for him to get back on the phone,' she said. Juan Thompson, in the next room, heard the bang, but thought that it was just a book falling.

According to the sheriff's report, Thompson's body was found in a chair by the kitchen table. On the table was a typewriter in which a single sheet of paper had been lined up. The last written word of the writer of *Fear and Loathing in Las Vegas* will in all likelihood puzzle literary experts for years to come. In the centre of the page was typed the word 'counsellor'.

 ## THE FUNERAL

The Thompson family cancelled plans for a public funeral in favour of a private ceremony. A wake, attended by Jann Wenner, Jack Nicholson, Benicio del Toro, Johnny Depp, Sean Penn and Ralph Steadman, was held in Aspen, two weeks after his suicide.

On 20 August 2005, Thompson's ashes were fired from a cannon atop a 153-foot-high tower across the Colorado Valley. The cannon, designed by Thompson and Ralph Steadman in the 1970s, was in the shape of a double-thumbed fist, clutching a peyote button. Bob Dylan's *Mr Tambourine Man*, his favourite song, was played during the proceedings. Amongst the 280 who attended the ceremony were unsuccessful Democrat presidential candidate Senator John Kerry, former Senator and equally unsuccessful Democrat presidential candidate George McGovern, actors Sean Penn, Josh Hartnett and Bill Murray, singers Lyle Lovett and John Oates and *60 Minutes* correspondent Ed Bradley, who would himself die the following year.

POST MORTEM

- A number of shots heard around the time that Thompson's body was discovered can be explained by the fact that, after finding his father dead, Juan Thompson walked out of the house and fired three shotgun blasts into the air, later saying he had done it 'to mark the passing of my father'.

- A letter, described by family and police as a suicide note, was delivered to Thompson's wife four days prior to his death. It was headed 'Football Season is Over' and read: 'No More Games. No More Bombs. No More Walking. No More Fun. No More Swimming. 67. That is 17 years past 50. 17 more than I needed or wanted. Boring. I am always bitchy. No Fun — for anybody. 67. You are getting Greedy. Act your old age. Relax — This won't hurt.'

- Thompson's friend and collaborator Ralph Steadman revealed after the suicide that Thompson had told him twenty-five years previously 'that he would feel real trapped if he didn't know that he could commit suicide at any moment'.

THE CONSPIRACY THEORY

- It is rumoured that, at the time of his suicide, Thompson was working on two incendiary stories. The first claimed that 9/11 was caused not by planes crashing into the World Trade Centre. On the contrary, he claimed, explosives in the foundations had been used to bring down the twin towers. Alternatively, it was reported that he had discovered evidence of a paedophile ring in Washington, and had evidence implicating senior US politicians. Was Thompson murdered because he knew too much about one or both of these stories and was about to expose them?

- There was something odd about the gun Thompson used to kill himself. In his report, Deputy Ron Ryan noted that the semi-automatic Smith & Wesson 645 found next to Thompson's body was in an unusual condition. There was a spent shell casing, but although there were six bullets left in the gun's clip, there was no bullet in the firing chamber, as there should have been under normal circumstances. However, a spent bullet was found in the stove hood behind the body.

- Thompson is reported to have telephoned a friend the night before his death, sounding scared. He told him about the World Trade Centre story and claimed that someone was out to stop him publishing it. 'They're gonna make it look like suicide,' he is reported to have said.

— ANDY WARHOL —

'Dying is the most embarrassing thing that can ever happen to you,' wrote Andy Warhol in his last book, *America*, 'because someone's got to take care of all your details ... someone's got to take care of the body, make the funeral arrangements, pick out the casket and the service and the cemetery and the clothes for you to wear and get someone to style you and put on the make-up. You'd like to help them, and most of all you'd like to do the whole thing yourself, but you're dead so you can't.'

On 22 January 1987, just under a month before it would become redundant, the extraordinary silver-grey wig of Andy Warhol made an appearance at the Credito Valtellinese Gallery in Milan, where an exhibition of his *Last Supper* series was opening to great acclaim. Televison lights lit up the crowds of people who filled the Palazzo della Stellina in expectation of seeing the artist. Despite the glamour and glitz, however, all was not well and Andy uncharacteristically retired to his suite in the Principe e Savoia Hotel well before midnight. He was in great pain and languished in his room for the remaining two days of his stay in Italy.

The pain came from enlarged gallstones from which he had been suffering for some time. Towards the end of 1986 he had been warned that they had become so enlarged that failure to have them removed could endanger his life. Andy, however, had a paranoid fear of hospitals and refused to acknowledge the problem for fear it would mean hospitalisation. Now, the pain was becoming more than he could bear. He was even curtailing his social life and, for Andy Warhol, that was unheard of.

He had recently been receiving treatment to remove his facial lines from a dermatologist, Dr Karen Burke, and on 14 February, he turned to her for help, pleading for the addictive pain relief drug Demerol to ease his condition. Burke refused to supply him with the drug and, instead, told him she would give him the much weaker Tylenol with some codeine but even then only on condition that he went to see another physician, Dr Clement Barone, for a sonogram on his right side. Still the artist demurred.

He spent the weekend of 14 and 15 February in bed but felt no improvement. So, he decided to try a *shiatsu* massage from Linda Li of Li Chiropractic Healing Arts Clinic. But this failed to provide him with the relief he sought and, if anything, made the pain even worse.

On the Tuesday, he was booked to do a catwalk show with the great jazz trumpeter Miles Davis, at The Tunnel, a recently opened New York club. Kept waiting in extreme pain in a cold dressing room for an hour before he went on, Andy still managed to put on a good show, clowning around with Davis, but collapsing into the arms of his friend Stuart Pivar when he left the stage, gasping: 'I feel like I'm gonna die!'

Next afternoon, Andy finally gave in and went to see his doctor, Denton Cox, where another sonogram confirmed Karen Burke's diagnosis. Cox informed him that his gallbladder was seriously infected and in danger of becoming gangrenous. He told him he would have to have it removed. On Thursday, another sonogram persuaded Andy that he finally had to do something, especially as he had caught a chill that was making his condition even worse.

On Friday 20 February, Andy's diary showed an appointment to act as a model at the New York Academy of Art. This was hastily cancelled and he checked into the New York Hospital under the alias 'Bob Robert', having had the alias he had first jokingly suggested – 'Barbara' – turned down. On his admittance form he listed his next of kin as his assistant Fred Hughes. It is an indication of his obsessive nature that when asked for his Blue Cross number – his health insurance number – Andy knew it by heart. The operation was to take place on Saturday and he would be out of hospital the next day. No one was to know, not even his closest family.

The operation lasted from 8.45 until 12.10 p.m. It went well and there were no complications. After spending three hours in the recovery room, he was wheeled into a private room on the twelfth floor of the part of the hospital known as Baker Pavilion. There, he was to be cared for not by a team of staff nurses but by a private duty nurse called Min Chou. The doctors examining him found everything to be proceeding normally and Andy was reported to be in good spirits, passing the time watching television and gossiping on the phone to his housekeeper, Paige Powell.

At eleven that night, Min Chou reported to the chief surgical resident that Andy's blood pressure was stable. However, at 5.45 next morning, his pulse suddenly weakened and he began to turn blue. Min Chou desperately tried to wake him but, unable to do so, called for help. For the next forty-five minutes doctors tried to revive him, even inserting a tube down his throat to ease his breathing, but by then, rigor mortis had set in.

At 6.21 a.m. on 22 February 1987, Andy Warhol was pronounced dead.

He had been famous for slightly more than fifteen minutes and in hospital he had kept his wig on at all times, even during the operation.

 ## THE FUNERAL

A viewing was held at the Thomas P. Kunsak Funeral Home in Pittsburgh. Andy wore a black cashmere suit, a paisley tie, a platinum wig and sunglasses. In his hands he held a small prayer book and a red rose. His casket was made of bronze, with gold-plated rails and white upholstery.

The funeral service took place at the Holy Ghost Byzantine Catholic Church, his coffin covered with white roses and asparagus ferns. He was buried in St John Divine Cemetery in Bethnel Park, Pittsburgh. Before the casket was lowered, Paige Powell dropped the latest issue of his magazine *Interview*, an *Interview* T-shirt and a bottle of Estée Lauder perfume into the grave.

There was a memorial service on 1 April at Manhattan's St Patrick's Cathedral at which Yoko Ono delivered a eulogy. After the service, the guests, including artists Roy Lichtenstein and Keith Haring, singer Liza Minelli and actor Don Johnson, enjoyed lunch at the Diamond Horseshoe during which Velvet Underground recordings played in the background. *Factory* technician and photographer Billy Name drew band members Lou Reed and John Cale into conversation with each other, easing the tension that had existed between them since their musical break-up. The result was their collaboration *Songs for Drella*, a tribute to Andy Warhol, which was released in April 1990 and which eventually led to the Velvets getting back together.

☠ POST MORTEM

- The District Attorney investigated his death but decided that there was no evidence of criminal irresponsibility. However, an investigation by the New York State Department of Health concluded that 'the active medical staff of the hospital did not assure the maintenance of the proper quality of all medication and treatment provided to the patient'. The Warhol estate brought a wrongful-death lawsuit against the hospital that was settled out of court for $3 million. The money went to Warhol's two brothers as part of a deal to guarantee that they would not contest Andy's will in which he had left them only $250,000.

- The courts conservatively estimated that Andy Warhol's estate was worth over half a billion dollars: $509,979,278, to be precise. This figure was contested by the Warhol Foundation and was subsequently reduced to $228 million – a lower estimate benefited the estate as it meant they would pay lower legal fees and would not have to dole out so much in charitable grants. Bizarrely, to obtain the lesser valuation, the estate argued in court that Warhol was not as great an artist as experts believed him to be. Art dealer André Emmerich testified for the Foundation that Warhol's work was likely to fade into obscurity because the subjects of his paintings – Marilyn Monroe, Elvis Presley and so on – would eventually be forgotten.

- On 3 May 1988, an auction of Andy's effects at Sotheby's was the largest single collection the 250-year-old auction house had ever sold, with sixty thousand people viewing it over a ten-day period. People paid fortunes for even insignificant items, including his collection of cookie jars. The auction raised a phenomenal $25,313,238.

— DENNIS WILSON —

He was the pretty one of the Beach Boys, but Dennis Wilson was also famously – and ironically – the only member of the group that rode on an early sixties wave of surf music who actually enjoyed surfing.

Following the glory years of teen adulation, however, his life had held nothing but disappointment. He had become entangled with Charles Manson and his murderous followers and then his film debut, starring alongside Warren Oates and James Taylor in the road movie *Two Lane Blacktop*, had failed to set the world on fire. Unfortunately, the same could be said about his solo album *Pacific Ocean Boulevard*, which received favourable reviews but failed to sell. Sadly, he became addicted to women, drugs and booze, each feeding on the other. It became so bad that the other Beach Boys told him if he did not clean up they would ban him from touring with them. But he needed the money the tours would bring. His lifestyle had become extravagant and he had been spending around $600,000 a year on fancy cars, diamonds and furs for the numerous women in his life.

Shortly before Christmas 1983, Dennis was yet again trying to tackle his demons when he checked into rehab at St John's

Hospital and Health Center in Santa Monica. He was drinking a bottle of vodka a day by this time and lacing that with a liberal daily intake of cocaine. Doctors there put him on a five-day course of Librium to try to stabilise him so that he could begin the effective twenty-one-day detox programme they ran. On Christmas Day, he walked out of the hospital, but early the next morning he checked into the Daniel Freeman Marina Hospital in Marina Del Rey. Next day, he checked out again and met up with his current wife – he married six times – Shawn Love, allegedly the illegitimate daughter of his cousin and fellow Beach Boy Mike Love.

It was a pity, because his business manager had promised Dennis he would buy back for him his 62-foot yacht *Harmony* if he could stay sober for thirty days. He had once lived on the yacht and had loved it almost as much as the women in his life. Short of cash in 1980, however, he had reluctantly been forced to sell it.

Dennis spent the night of 27 December at Marina Del Rey with a friend, Colleen McGovern, on the *Emerald*, a 52-foot sloop owned by his friend Bill Oster. Waking at nine, he started this day the way he had started all the others recently – he drank vodka. Then, he and Oster rowed around the harbour, visiting friends and buying cigarettes. They ate turkey sandwiches on Oster's boat and, by all accounts, Dennis was happy, having a good time.

He was also pretty drunk – the drinking had carried on through the morning and lunch.

After lunch, he slept for a while before visiting a friend, Lathiel Morris, who lived on a nearby houseboat. They talked about him getting his boat back and about Dennis' forthcoming divorce. Talking about relationships, Dennis told Morris: 'I'm lonesome. I'm lonesome all the time.'

At three in the afternoon, Dennis was diving into the harbour at the spot where the *Harmony* had once been moored. He had thrown stuff overboard at various times during his relationships and was keen to recover some of it. The first thing he brought up was a picture of an ex-wife that he had tossed overboard during an argument. But the water was cold and he was clad only in cut-off jeans and a facemask. After about twenty minutes he climbed out of the water, shivering violently. After warming up again and wolfing down a sandwich, however, he jumped back in. It was now around four in the afternoon.

About fifteen minutes later, Oster saw him blow a few bubbles and swim towards the yacht's dinghy. He was swimming quietly and Oster presumed he was trying to hide from them. But, when he failed to emerge from the water again, they began to become concerned.

Oster flagged down a passing harbour patrol boat and told them of his concerns, but he was still convinced that Dennis was playing a trick on them and had clambered ashore out of sight and even now was seated at a nearby bar drinking vodka. They set out to find him, but he was nowhere to be seen. Meanwhile, divers began to explore the waters around the *Emerald*.

They found him at about 5.30 using a long pole to probe the bottom of the harbour. He was thirty-nine years old and surf was up.

 ## THE FUNERAL

As with most things involving the brothers Wilson and the Beach Boys, there were bitter arguments about how Dennis would be buried. His wife Shawn wanted to have him buried at sea, but his brother Carl made plans for him to be buried at Inglewood Cemetery beside the brothers' father Murray, who had died ten years previously. Shawn won, as the coroner had to legally release Dennis' body to his next of kin, who was his wife.

Three days after his death, a thirty-minute funeral service was held for him at a cemetery chapel in Inglewood. Present were Dennis' mother Audree; the remaining Beach Boys and close associates; Shawn; his first wife Carol Freedman; and her son Scott, twenty-one, from a prior marriage, and Dennis' oldest child, sixteen-year-old Jennifer; his second wife Barbara Charren and their sons, Carl and Michael, aged twelve and eleven; and Karen Lamm, whom Dennis married twice in the late 1970s. After the funeral service a wake was held at the house of one of the Beach Boys' management team.

Mike Love, a strict teetotal vegetarian, turned up with four bottles of the most expensive champagne he could find because, he said, 'Dennis would have wanted it that way.' He played basketball with Brian Wilson that afternoon and they discussed writing a song for Dennis.

On 4 January, three boats containing the Wilson family and friends put to sea with Dennis Wilson's body and he was put to rest in the place he loved best.

 ## POST MORTEM

When they told Charles Manson in prison that Dennis Wilson had drowned, he commented: 'Dennis Wilson was killed by my shadow because he took my music and changed the words from my soul.'

— NATALIE WOOD —

In autumn 1981, Natalie Wood was starring in a science fiction film called *Brainstorm* with Christopher Walken. She and her husband, Robert Wagner – she was in her second marriage to the *Hart to Hart* actor – invited Walken to spend Thanksgiving weekend with them on board their 55-foot cabin cruiser, the *Splendor*. They planned to spend the holiday weekend cruising off the Los Angeles coast of California.

On the first day of the cruise, 27 November, their one-man crew, Captain Dennis Davern, piloted the boat to Catalina Island where they put down anchor. Waking from their naps before Wagner, Wood and Walken sailed the yacht's dinghy ashore and drank for a couple of hours in a Catalina restaurant where Wagner later joined them for dinner and more drinks. They returned to the *Splendor* at 10 p.m., already quite drunk, and resumed their drinking onboard.

Wagner's complaints that his wife spent too much time on her acting career and not enough time looking after their children turned into an argument. Walken sided with Wood and as the drinks flowed, the argument raged into the night.

Next day, 28 November, the *Splendor* put down anchor at Isthmus Cove. The trio dined that evening at the Harbor Reef Restaurant, beginning at four in the afternoon with several bottles of champagne and causing a disturbance in the restaurant, where, it is claimed, Natalie had been openly flirting with Walken. Leaving the restaurant very drunk, they clambered aboard their small dinghy and returned to the *Splendor*. Things become unclear at this point, but what is certain is that as Captain Davern began to shut the boat down for the night, the three continued to party.

At around 12.20 a.m., Davern noticed that the boat's dinghy was missing. He knew that Natalie often took it to view the evening sky away from the boat and presumed that this was what had happened. But, when she failed to return, Davern became worried and informed Wagner who immediately jumped into a second dinghy and went to look for her.

The coroner later suggested a likely version of the night's tragic events. Wood had indeed gone out in the dinghy but had then slipped and fallen into the water. Desperately, she had tried to crawl up the sides of the rubber dinghy, but the heavy coat she was wearing as protection against the night chill, sodden with water, now weighed thirty to forty pounds and prevented her from clambering into the boat. As she struggled to get into the dinghy, it had started to drift slowly out into the harbour. Becoming frightened, she had begun to scream but her yells had been drowned out by the noise of a loud stereo on a boat nearby. She had grabbed the side of the dinghy and had begun to steer it towards the shore but eventually she succumbed to the cold and died, shrouded in her nightgown and red down coat.

She was forty-three years old.

 ## THE FUNERAL

Natalie Wood's gardenia-clad casket was buried in Westwood Village Memorial Park Cemetery in Los Angeles on 2 December 1981. Natasha, Natalie's eleven-year-old daughter, requested that diamond earrings be placed on her mother's ears and Robert Wagner insisted on burying her in a fox-fur coat that he had not yet given to her.

Numerous celebrities, including Sir Laurence Olivier, Rock Hudson, Gregory Peck and Elizabeth Taylor, attended the funeral, alongside Robert Wagner and Christopher Walken.

 ## POST MORTEM

- The official coroner's report states that a private searcher who located the dinghy says that the key was in the ignition, which was in the off position. The gear was in neutral and the oars tied down. From this account, it would appear that the boat had not even been used.

- Sources close to Robert Wagner insist that Natalie Wood drowned when she slipped into the water after becoming annoyed by the incessant pounding of the dinghy tied up on the side of the yacht.

- Some reports say that Wagner and Walken had a violent argument that night, that Natalie tried to leave the yacht and accidentally fell overboard. A woman on shore later said she heard cries for help in the water and heard other voices saying they were coming. Wagner, Walken and the captain of the *Splendor* all deny this. The coroner pointed out that Wood was legally intoxicated at the time of her death and there were unexplained marks and bruises on her body.
- Her body required cosmetic work before she could be buried.

INDEX